Boom

Boom

Visions and Insights for Creating Wealth in the 21st Century

Frank Vogl

James Sinclair

IRWIN
Professional Publishing

Chicago • Bogatá • Boston • Buenos Aires • Caracas
London • Madrid • Mexico City • Sydney • Toronto

Irwin Professional Book Team

Editor-in-chief: *Jeffrey A. Krames*
Senior marketing manager: *Tiffany Chenevert Dykes*
Project editor: *Denise Santor-Mitzit*
Production supervisor: *Lara Feinberg*
Assistant manager, desktop services: *Jon Christopher*
Compositor: *Douglas & Gayle, Ltd.*
Typeface: *11/13 Garamound*
Printer: *Book Press, Inc.*

■▼■ Times Mirror
M Higher Education Group

ISBN: 0-7863-0527-4

Printed in the United States of America
1 2 3 4 5 6 7 8 9 0 BP 2 1 0 9 8 7 6 5

To
Barbara, and Emily
and to
Christine, Michelle, Marlene, Julia, and Marc

Preface

A new era of economic growth is unfolding in most of the countries of the world, which will gather momentum as we enter the 21st century. An Industrial Revolution is taking place in the emerging market countries. Hundreds of millions of people, perhaps billions, will benefit and rise from poverty to form new middle classes. Supplying their consumer demands and building the infrastructure for their economies—particularly in *Asia,* and concurrently in *Latin America, Africa, and Eastern Europe*—represents an outstanding business opportunity.

The boom is stimulated by the steady growth and low-inflation policies now being seen in the United States and in other leading industrial countries, as well as by policies in dozens of emerging market economies that encourage investment, savings, and price stability. It is supported by social policies that are raising educational and health levels in many parts of the Third World. And it will be strengthened as markets for all manner of goods and services in developing countries are being linked by technology, telecommunications, and multinational investors.

The media too often dwell on the bad news and many analysts pounce on a crisis, such as the one that hit Mexico in late 1994/early 1995, to promote gloomy predictions. We have written this book to build a broader appreciation of the extraordinary time in which we are living, the bright economic prospects ahead, and the challenges that are posed by a new era of global business. The smartest investors are already positioning themselves to take full advantage of the boom, as are many multinational corporations. They know that the maximization of profit will increasingly depend on going global and they recognize that the fastest rates of economic growth in coming years will not be in the United States, Germany, and Japan, but in Third World countries. They also understand that business conditions in almost all markets will be more competitive than ever before.

The economic boom will have political consequences. In the leading industrial countries, fears of the competition posed by the newly emerging industrial economies will unleash protectionist pressures. These must be firmly resisted. The surest path to prosperity rests in the advanced industrial nations continuing to demonstrate the benefits of open borders for global trade and investment to all peoples and all nations. The emerging economies should not be seen as threats, but rather as positive challenges, forcing corporations to become smarter and more efficient.

The boom will also have geopolitical consequences for the most advanced industrial nations, who have dominated the world stage in this century. They will now have to learn to share their influence and dominance with China, India, and the other fast growing, emerging market economies. Meanwhile, within the Third World countries the boom will also have political impact, as the growing new middle classes seek a greater voice in politics and promote greater pressures for democracy.

All of these political changes do contain within them risks to the boom scenario that we outline. On balance we see firm grounds for optimism, but the risks need to be considered. Trade protectionism is one such risk. Another is the possibility that economic growth in some emerging economies will be undermined by too much public spending on military arms and too little on civilian infrastructure. In some countries, populist, nationalist leaders may push aside politicians who favor democracy, thereby stunting the development of free enterprise.

As we stress in this book, we are particularly sensitive to the threat posed to the boom scenario by corruption. From Russia to China to India, the new era of free enterprise that is emerging is being accompanied by extensive abuse of public office for private gain. This in turn undermines human rights, endangers the establishment of democracy, creates waste, and threatens economic growth. We do, however, see many positive actions being taken to counter the corruption trend, and we believe there are many approaches that business needs to take in going global to deal with this menace. We stress in the book the vital priority for corporations to seek partnerships in emerging economies, to act transparently, and to always remember that their reputation is their most valuable asset. In the context of our approaches to the corruption issue, we are particularly appreciative of the endorsement our book has received from one of the true champions of this fight, Nobel laureate Oscar Arias Sanchez.

The complexity of operating globally is a theme of several chapters in this book. Entrepreneurs, managers, and portfolio investors alike must all plan for an era of growth where emerging markets rise rapidly as profit centers; where the face of the corporate labor force becomes much more multicultural; and where national borders become less significant in planning strategies. To win, investors must be able to accurately determine which companies and which markets are adapting best and fastest to the new era. At the corporate level this means redefining goals and approaches to doing business, building global networks of contacts, securing vast amounts of business intelligence, and developing approaches to positioning themselves, their products, and their services in new markets. In short, whatever your business and your involvement in commerce and finance, or whatever your interest in understanding international developments, you will increasingly have to adopt a global state of mind.

The first part of this book is based on a great deal of research and personal travel. We could not have put it together without drawing upon information published by many scholars, research organizations, and corporations. We have worked in recent years with Karl Sauvant and his team at the Division on Transnational Corporations and Investment of the United Nations Conference on Trade and Development in Geneva. Their studies of multinational corporations and critical issues facing the managements of these corporations is outstanding, and we are grateful that we have been allowed to quote from their published work. The second part of this book draws on many sources. For basic data we are indebted, in particular, to the work published by both the United Nations Development Program and the World Bank. With regard to corruption, we have been privileged to work with many individuals who are devoting their time to efforts to curb this cancer and who have educated us, especially Peter Eigen and his colleagues involved with Transparency International, a not-for-profit organization.

The points we make and the conclusions we draw regarding managing in the new business era are largely based on our personal experiences over the last 30 years in running, advising, reporting, and otherwise working with multilateral organizations. We are most indebted to executives at 3M, American Express, Ford Motor Company, The Reader's Digest Association, Inc., and the WPP Group, who read parts of this manuscript and corrected some of our errors.

We are also grateful to friends who helped us define our goals with this book at an early stage, notably independent management consultant Matthew Whalen, and Loyd Pettigrew, Professor of Communications at the University of South Florida. We owe a great debt to our business partners, especially our colleagues at Sutton Resources Ltd., and to our many friends and business associates in Tanzania who have taught us so much. Then, this book would not have been possible without the support and wisdom of our office colleagues Maria Fasano and Michael Tesoro, our literary agent Robert Ducas, our editor Elizabeth McDonell, and the team at Irwin Professional Publishing, especially editor-in-chief, Jeffrey Krames and project editor, Denise Santor-Mitzit. Most of all we thank our wives and children for their support and patience with us as we worked on *BOOM*.

We believe that the early years of the 21st century will see many hundreds of millions of people wrestle free from the clutches of poverty as economic growth moves ahead. Our hope is that this phenomenon will be widely recognized for what it really is: the dawn of a new economic era where the world's economies will be more closely entwined than ever in history and thereby open unprecedented opportunities, not just for business, but for human development and for cooperation between nations.

Frank Vogl
James Sinclair

Contents

Part I

BOOM and the New Industrial Revolution

1

The New Industrial Revolution

B y 2025, China could be the world's largest economy, having pushed the United States into second place. India could be in the top five, with an economy as large, or almost as large, as that of Japan and Germany. Several other leading Asian nations, along with possibly Mexico, Brazil, and Argentina in Latin America, could have bigger economies than many of the nations of Western Europe. Across the Third World, two to three billion people will have emerged from poverty to enjoy middle-class affluence. As we begin a new century, we are also standing at the dawn of a new era, a second Industrial Revolution that will be breathtaking in its scope, potential, and promise. Ahead lies a period of unprecedented economic growth: a boom that could last 30 years or more.

> "By 2025, China could be the world's largest economy."

This new era will generate not only enormous growth around the world; it will also create huge political changes in the emerging nations, as economic advances unleash democratic pressures. It will be a more complex world, too, as these countries seek greater global political power and force heads of states, public policy experts, and businesspeople to think anew about international relations and international commercial opportunities.

We must recognize that the Third World is becoming a most powerful engine of global economic growth. Its role in stimulating international expansion of trade, business, and portfolio investment is growing with rising momentum. The Third World will be the prime location for new investments in infrastructure, from roads and ports to power systems and whole new telecommunications services. It will be the location of dramatically rising cash flows of mutual fund, pension fund, and individual investment cash from North America, Japan, and Eastern Europe. The first Industrial Revolution, starting in England at the end of the 18th Century, produced extraordinary social progress for hundreds of millions of people in what we now call the advanced industrial countries, or First World. Now, in the second Industrial Revolution, the beneficiaries will be the vast numbers of peoples from the tips of the African and Latin American continents to the mountain peaks of Northern Asia.[1]

Industrialization is taking place at a furious pace, changing the face of the Third World and creating substantial increases in the incomes of billions of people. And, whereas the first Industrial Revolution was a long and drawn-out affair, the new one is zooming ahead at supersonic speed. According to *The Economist*:

> Over the years the pace of economic development seems to have quickened. The industrial revolution in the 18th and 19th centuries was a slow affair compared with growth rates today. Thanks to better communications, technology is now diffused more quickly than in the past. After the industrial revolution took hold in about 1780, Britain needed 58 years to double its real income per head; from 1839 America took 47 years to do the same; starting in 1885, Japan took 34 years; South Korea managed it in just 11 years from 1966; and, more recently still, China has done it in less than ten years.[2]

By 2025 the earth's population may exceed 9 billion people, more than two-thirds of whom will live in the Third World.[3] Perhaps one billion of these people will be homeless, malnourished, and desperate; they will challenge our humanitarian sensitivity. There may be another one to two billion people who are barely better off, who may exert massive migration pressures, and who may threaten our security. In addition, for the first time in history, vast numbers of people in the Third World will also enjoy living standards that will be higher than they could have ever dreamed possible. Billions of people are set on a course that will propel them from poverty to modest prosperity in the next two to three decades. They will create a new middle class within their societies, with new habits and expectations to match their income levels.

Supplying the needs of this new consumer class is the greatest business opportunity to open up since the post-World War II years (1945-1970), when today's advanced industrial nations rose from the rubble and exhaustion of the war to become the most affluent societies ever constructed. Western businesses are creating these new Third World opportunities by investing tens of billions of dollars in the transfer of technologies and by implementing strategies to integrate the world into efficient markets. As the dynamics of global economics continue to change, so major corporations will continue to be at the core, both as its agents of change and as its victims. Those that see and seize the opportunities will win, those that fail to recognize the new intensity of global competition will lose.

> "The emerging middle class represents the greatest business opportunity since the post-World War II years"

To understand the phenomenon of the unfolding Industrial Revolution and how Western businesses can participate in it, we must first understand the central reasons for this new growth. In the remainder of this chapter, we will set the stage for this discussion by looking at the forces behind this Revolution: advances in education and science, technology, economics and politics, and trade and investment. In chapters two and three, we will continue to explore the boom from a global perspective, looking at doing business in the boom era and at its capital needs.

Advances in Education and Science

The changes that are now unfolding in the Third World are largely due to an influx of massive, successful investments, specifically in the areas of education and science. In education, the creation of literate populations from China to Chile, from Taiwan to Tanzania, represents the greatest force for positive change on the planet in our era. Never before have so many people in the world been able to read and write. This change is the foundation for vast increases in productivity in almost all societies.

The economic dynamism so widespread in China, for example, has been due in large measure to the intense priority given by local, regional, and national authorities, as well as families and communities, to education. Following the Cultural Revolution, 1966–76, which destroyed most learning institutions in the country, the government once again began placing exceptional emphasis on investing in education. In 1978, there were less than 500 institutions of higher education in all of China; a decade later the total exceeded 1,100. Elsewhere in Asia, Taiwan, Korea, and Singapore provide fine examples of how investing heavily in schools boosts the productive potential of the poor and leads to rapid economic payoffs. Developing countries across the world are applying this lesson.

In Africa, education has played a major role in the recent move toward political stability. For instance, after Tanzania gained political independence from Britain in 1961, the Tanzanian government started major initiatives in education, and they attached the highest importance to building a school system to secure a common language, basic skills for all citizens, and a sense of nationhood. As a result, Tanzania has become one of the most stable and open democracies in Eastern and Southern Africa.[4]

Overall, in the past two decades, primary school enrollment throughout the Third World has increased from an average of less than 25 percent to 40 percent. Most significantly, the secondary enrollment ratio for girls increased from 17 percent in 1970 to 36 percent in 1990, according to World Bank data. This is the first era in history in which many poor nations are recognizing the productive potential of women and, accordingly, adjusting social and education policies to provide women with greater opportunities.

In science, stunningly successful investments in the Third World have reduced the dangers of humanitarian disasters and set the base for dramatic productivity gains. The "green revolution" of the 1960s and 1970s boosted crop yields so formidably that it enabled India to escape the horror of frequent periods of massive food shortages and starvation and become food self-sufficient. In the mid-1960s, the world was shocked by the suffering caused by famine in India. Less than a generation later this country had become a food exporter.

Furthermore, the development of "super rice" in Asia may dramatically boost yields in scores of nations and lead to huge improvements in diets for hundreds of millions of people.[5] Scientific breakthroughs like super rice have fundamentally opened the door to the prospect of global food supply adequacy. In 1965, only about 25 developing countries met their daily per capita calorie requirements, widely viewed by the United Nations as the minimum necessary for decent health. In contrast, by 1990 that figure had doubled to 50 countries.

Similar scientific advances are evident on the health front with the development of new vaccines and the implementation of vast immunization programs. For example, in the Volta River basin in West Africa, whole villages were once destroyed by "river blindness." Now, regular spraying of the area and distribution of vaccines has all but eradicated the disease, and thousands of poor people in the region no longer fear going blind.[6]

Moreover, nearly all developing countries have succeeded in wiping out smallpox, reducing infant mortality, and increasing life expectancy. Over the past three decades, average life expectancy has increased by more than one third, with 23 developing countries achieving life expectancy of 70 years or more. In the same period, mortality rates for children under five have been cut in half. Encouraging progress has also been made in family planning, and family sizes have dropped throughout Asia and in parts of Latin America. Progress is also being made in some African countries.

While the scale of illness in many Third World countries is still high compared with the leading industrial nations, and new diseases such as AIDS continue to pose new threats, the overall levels of human health improvement in many of the poorer countries in the last 30 years has been extraordinary.

Technology and a Borderless World

Myriad new technologies are playing an equally important role in securing quantum jumps in Third World productivity and prosperity. They are changing every aspect of international economic and

political activity. Indeed, new technologies and the major corporations behind them are binding national economies together to the
point where, according to Harvard Business School Professor Theodore
Leavitt, they are driving "the world toward a single, converging com-
monality . . . homogenizing markets everywhere."

In short, suggests Fumio Sato, president and CEO of Toshiba
Corporation, technology is creating a "borderless economy" that
is generating breath-
taking ambitions.[7] For
example, Bill Gates, co-
founder of Microsoft
Corporation, and Craig
McCaw, founder of
McCaw Cellular Com-
munications (since
merged with AT&T), created Teledesic Corporation with a plan to
launch 840 communication satellites to wire the world. At a cost
of $9 billion, Teledesic intends to launch the satellites just after
the year 2000 to create a system to carry interactive voice, data,
and video services. If Teledesic realizes its potential, there will
not be a corner of the world that cannot obtain instant information from anywhere else on the planet.[8]

> "Technology is creating
> a 'borderless economy.'"

Technology is also accelerating the pace at which capital and
information moves from one nation to another, providing new opportunities for investors. As Brookings Institute scholar Wolfgang H.
Reinicke noted in 1994 in *The Brookings Review*, "Technology now
travels the globe practically unfettered—through licensed production agreements, co-development programs, subcontracting, joint ventures, mergers and acquisitions, and exchanges of data and personnel."

According to Nobel Prize–winning economist Milton Friedman, the technological revolution in computers and telecommunications has made it possible "to a far greater extent than at any
time in the world's history, for a company to locate anywhere,[9] to
use resources from anywhere, to produce a product that can be sold
anywhere." Friedman sees technology coming together with politics
to produce exceptional change. He stated that the fall of communism has created a kind of political revolution, like that which
embraces China, with the result that:

"Throughout the world, probably something like two-and-a-half billion people have now been put together in a new interrelationship with the advanced countries of the world. This offers the world an enormous opportunity, the opportunity of a major industrial revolution comparable in magnitude to that which occurred a few hundred years ago.[10]

As the new technologies weaken the power of national borders and sovereign governments (no official regulatory authority or politician can stop the transitional telephone call, the CNN broadcast, or the wiring of billions of dollars between markets across the globe in split seconds), so increasing amounts of all forms of business will move from a national to an international base. And, as the number of multinational companies grows and their skills improve, so the world economy will become more integrated. New, efficient production and distribution systems will emerge and contribute to rising affluence for a huge segment of the world's population.

Economic Advancement and Political Change

The transformation of the emerging economies into democracies with middle classes that are educated and concerned with securing more open political systems will strengthen many countries. But the evolution on this front will not always be easy. The fact is, digesting the intense economic and political changes now occurring will be difficult for many societies. Internal political disruption within some of the leading emerging economies is bound to surface, primarily because of the inability of some governments to cope with the demands of an emerging mass middle class and with the financial opportunities that economic dynamism offers.

The impact of this new economic era on political life will be profound. The leading industrial nations (namely the G-7 countries[11]) have dominated politics and global economies. Now they will have to learn to share their influence and dominance with China, India, and the other former Third World countries that are trailblazing the new economics. It will be difficult for many of the advanced industrial nations—and for individuals and corporations within them—to come to terms with a multipolar world, where prosperity and high levels of sophisticated economic activity are simultaneously in evidence in a multitude of locations.

Western multinational corporations will also have to adjust to new ways of doing business. Many of these multinationals have long been used to dominating new markets and economies. In today's multipolar world, however, they will need to accept the reality of full equality of, and partnerships with, foreign individuals and interests.

Many emerging economies that have done remarkably well in recent years through their own initiative are still frequently treated by Western governments and Western multinational companies as colonial subjects. This must change. As Malaysian Finance Minister Anwar Ibrahim declared of Britain, they must learn that "developing countries, including a country led by a brown Muslim, have the ability to manage their affairs successfully."[12]

While most Third World nations will succeed and move along the positive course described in this book, there will be important exceptions. Some governments will make a mess of economic management. Some may be governed by dangerous dictators, or be trapped in political chaos. In fact, no threat to the boom scenario is greater than that posed by corruption—the abuse of public office for private gain. Corruption is widespread and may get worse as the tempo of economic growth increases and as fundamental changes take place in the structures of economies. In some countries, such as Nigeria and Zaire, corruption has already become so chronic that is has smashed huge economic potential. In other countries, particularly in the former Soviet Union, corruption is creating intense turmoil and in-fighting. The ethical standards of politicians, civil servants, and major businesses (including foreign corporations) will be monitored ever more intensively.[13]

Trade and Investment

As the boom scenario unfolds, a central challenge for Western political leaders will be to find the means to ensure that the countries run by extreme nationalists and autocrats do not damage the fabric of an increasingly prosperous economic system embracing the overwhelming majority of nations. Part of the challenge for the most advanced industrial nations is to continue demonstrating the benefits of open borders for global trade and investment to all peoples and all nations. Encouraging global commerce on fair, competitive terms is an imperative.

Trade and investment rank alongside education, science, and technological innovation in building the framework for the new Industrial Revolution. Efforts by governments to forge global trade treaties to reduce protectionism and open markets (i.e., the multilateral trade liberalization agreements under GATT, the General Agreement on Tariffs and Trade[14]), as well as similar initiatives to stimulate international capital movement and investment, have enhanced opportunities for emerging countries.

Despite fears often expressed by some politicians and labor leaders that the rise of the developing economies will lead to the demise of the economies of the industrial countries, the pressure to continue to strengthen free trade and investment has been sustained. Most leaders around the world have understood that global integration is a plus sum economic game. Indeed, it is essential in a world that Stanford University Professor Paul Krugman asserts is "a complex web of feedback relationships—not a simple chain of one-way effects. In this global economic system, wages prices, trade, and investments flows are outcomes, not givens."[15]

The emerging boom in the Third World today is frequently being depicted through the lens of financial journalists, who have increasingly concentrated their focus on new stock markets. These reporters have tracked the flows of tens of billions of dollars in the first half of the 1990s into the markets of countries that in the 1980s were widely seen as financial basket cases, or at least far too immature to interest Wall Street financiers.

The ability of many Third World governments to pursue tough, reform-oriented economic policies and liberalize their economies to enable them to attract foreign investment and strengthen their own finances contributed to building a new climate. Foreign investors started to take notice, especially in the early years of this decade, when European, Japanese, and U.S. markets were offering relatively modest returns on investments.

Investing in some of these emerging stock markets became the height of fashion, as the media featured dashing mutual fund managers with a taste for Asia and Latin America as the new stars of our era. There must have been smiles all around at the House of Barings in London, one of the oldest investment banks in the world, when *Forbes* headlined a story in 1994 that read: "Barings' best buys: here's a rundown of which markets look hot and which look cold to its analysts."

But, in early 1995, Barings went bust, the victim of inadequate management controls over operations in its office in Singapore. A young trader at the most established investment bank in the U.K. took enormous advantage of the self-satisfaction of the top brass at Barings in London, who saw in emerging markets and new financial instruments only a golden path to ever-greater riches. They failed to understand how risky the new world of globally integrated finance and emerging markets was becoming.[16]

As with all fashions, many people got swept up without fully understanding what was happening. The herd instinct of the mutual fund investment industry was in full flight, as people who had barely ever visited the Third World now started to invest hundreds of millions of dollars of other peoples' cash in exotic and distant lands.

While some economists understood how profound the changes were in much of the Third World and started to accept the view that a major, long-term boom was in the making, many others believed that vast, short-term fortunes were certain. Thus, Wall Street speculators, often running huge mutual funds, were seemingly indiscriminate in pushing cash into markets as diverse as those of Turkey, India, Mexico, Venezuela, and Kenya.

Sometimes the investment managers pushed so much money into these countries that they did more harm than good, lulling governments into complacency that resulted in huge new inflation and massive increases in balance of payments deficits. Nowhere was this more evident than in Mexico. The country that in 1982 had defaulted on its foreign banks debts was the darling of the global investment community by 1992. In 1994, foreign investors poured billions of dollars into the Mexican stock market and Mexican bonds. The Mexican government was overconfident when it came to economics and was distracted by a presidential election, regional unrest, political assassinations, and new pressures for more democratic forms of government. By the end of the year, the balance of payments deficit was huge, the nation's foreign currency reserves were inadequate, and the peso was overvalued. A new government was elected, but it was nervous and inexperienced, and a crisis erupted—a crisis that was ended in part by record flows of funds from the U.S. government and other official public authorities abroad and in part by new, tough, economic programs.[17]

The events in Mexico, as well as similar developments in Turkey and Venezuela in 1994, gave the market speculators a rude awakening. These episodes underscored to international investors that they need to better understand the fundamental trends, the reasons why some countries were set to do well and others would fail.

The rash actions of short-term investors, the ignorance of many mutual fund managers, and the Mexican crisis have caused some people to conclude that the growth of emerging markets is a short-term wonder and largely a myth. This is arrant nonsense. This view neglects not only the massive changes in education, health, science, and technology, but also the direct corporate investment trends, infrastructure developments, reformed economic policies, and the rising incomes of hundreds of millions of people in the Third World. Put all of the changes together and you have the perfect stage for a long-term boom.

> "The stage is set for a long-term boom in emerging markets."

It is true that many Third World countries will slacken on the policy front at times; they may even suffer political volatility and economic recessions. As a result, these countries will disappoint investors who have plunged their savings into Third World stock markets. It is important to keep in mind that, as with any investment, a sense of perspective is essential. Highly mindful of this, George V. Grune, Chairman and former CEO of the Reader's Digest Association, Inc., has warned that:

We have to discipline ourselves to think more in a historical, long-range context than in the 'sound bite' version of events that we see on the evening news. I am concerned that after all the giddy optimism, global markets will materialize more slowly than we anticipate—and some of us may become disillusioned and draw back. This would shortchange our nation's competitiveness. It would also weaken the embryonic democratic trends around the world—and they are fragile enough as it is.[18]

The setbacks that will inevitably surface in some countries need to be understood as slowing, but not wrecking, the march to a new era of prosperity. There will be distractions to be sure, but, overall, the new century will bring brighter economic prospects for most of the planet's population than have ever been seen before.

2

Business' Crucial Roles in Building the Boom

I n the previous chapter, we asserted that a new Industrial Revolution is occurring in the countries we have known as the Third World. Advances in education and science, technology, economics, and politics have created a dynamic base for growth and international competitiveness in many countries. Leading corporations in these countries, together with rising numbers of multinational enterprises, are now creating enormous global business opportunities from this base. In short, globalization is here and it has happened, above all, because modernization and rapid economic growth are reaching high levels in many parts of the world simultaneously.

Will business be able to adjust to the dawning of this new industrial age and take full advantage of it? If the answer is yes, then the world economic outlook is bright. Much of this book is devoted to this response and to the reality that, to succeed, many business leaders must acquire new knowledge and learn new skills. They must formulate and pursue processes designed for a whole new era of economic activity.

There are good prospects that business leaders will succeed. A growing number of multinational corporations are already investing in the emerging economies on a substantial scale, thereby strengthening the forces for economic expansion. These investments are transferring not only cash to the emerging nations, but also vital technology and management know-how.

The framework for private sector investment in the Third World is the subject of this chapter. In it we look at the broad issues involved in the emergence of increasing numbers of multinational enterprises and at aspects of their leadership, at the transformation taking place in the "informal economies" of the Third World and at the approaches that host governments are taking to stimulate foreign direct investment and business development.

Becoming Multinational

First, the hard facts. There are approximately 37,000 parent companies with over 170,000 foreign affiliates in the universe of multinational enterprise today. These corporations account for annual sales in excess of $4.8 trillion.[1] The number of new multinational corporations being created each year is growing rapidly, as are the number of affiliated companies of the multinationals.

> "Daily global volume of currency trading now exceeds $1 trillion."

The multinational business arena is expanding in all business sectors. In finance, for example, daily global volume of currency trading now exceeds $1 trillion, while global trading in derivative financial instruments is now covering asset values in excess of $35 trillion.

All business will become more multinational. As the number of multinationals grows, so global investment will expand, support for sustained economic growth will deepen, and the prospects of rising affluence for most of the world's population will brighten. This optimistic perspective is based on the growth-promoting example that is being set by some of the largest and the most dynamic multinational corporations.

For instance, Ford Motor Company is building world cars—the same range of cars is being produced, assembled, and sold across the globe; The Reader's Digest Association, Inc., is selling more types of cultural products (from books to CDs, CD-Roms, and videos) in more languages to more countries; and News Corporation, under

THE WORLD'S LARGEST MULTINATIONAL CORPORATIONS
(ranked in terms of assets in 1992 in billions of U.S. dollars and in terms of total numbers of employees, listed below in thousands)

Company	Nationality and Industry	Foreign Assets	Total Assets	Sales	Employees
1 Royal Dutch Shell	U.K./Netherlands Petroleum	69.4	100.8	96.6	127
2 Exxon	U.S.A. Petroleum	48.2	85.0	115.7	95
3 IBM	U.S.A. Computers	45.7	86.7	64.5	143.9
4 General Motors	U.S.A. Motor vehicles/Parts	41.8	191.0	132.4	750.0
5 Hitachi	Japan Electronics	....	66.6	58.4	324.2
6 Matsushita Electric	Japan Electronics	....	74.4	60.8	252.1
7 Nestle	Switzerland Food	28.7	31.3	38.4	218.0
8 Ford Motor Co.	U.S.A. Automobiles	28.0	180.5	100.1	325.3
9 Alcatel Alsthom	France Electronics	....	44.4	30.7	203.0
10 General Electric	U.S.A. Electronics	24.2	192.9	57.1	231.0

Source: "The Top Transnational Corporations," from *World Investment Report 1994*, published August, 1994, by the United Nations Conference on Trade and Development.

the leadership of Rupert Murdoch, is investing vast sums in a global television network in which China is seen as the long-term lead market. Coca-Cola is focusing on the Third World for growth because, as its Chairman Robert C. Goizueta noted in his company's 1993 annual report, the evolution of the world's poorer citizens into consumers with disposable income is providing Coca-Cola "fresh access to three billion new potential consumers of our beverages around the globe."[2]

Operating a business in the global economy is far more complex than operating within a single national market. Transforming a corporation from a national entity (or one with just a few operations in a few countries) to a genuinely multinational enterprise challenges every aspect of corporate culture—every aspect of the way companies think of themselves and of the way their employees view their mission and business environment. The winners will be those who see the world as one large, fully integrated market.

> "Transforming a corporation into a genuinely multinational enterprise challanges every aspect of corporate culture."

Martin Sorrell of WPP Group plc exemplifies the type of vision business people need to remain competitive. For many people in the advertising industry, IBM's decision in May 1994 to fire most of its agencies and place all of its $500 million annual global advertising with one firm was a bombshell. But for Sorrell it was vindication. He had always planned and preached the concept of building a corporation strong and global enough to serve the total marketing needs of the largest world corporations. Over several years, he acquired some of the largest advertising companies on both sides of the Atlantic. He stuck with his global concept even when the world's leading economies fell into recession and his finances came under pressure. As the CEO of WPP Group plc, headquartered in London, he had long claimed that, in a shrinking world and one full of new technologies, the time would come when it made sense for multinational firms to think globally in their marketing. Nobody in the advertising world had Sorrell's vision and guts. His reward? WPP's subsidiary, Ogilvy & Mather Worldwide, won the IBM contract.[3]

Never before have opportunities in developing countries been more attractive for those who are willing, like Sorrell, to make the investment of time and money necessary to learn. And never before have so many businesses taken an interest in the global economic environment and been able to tap so much information to assist them in making the right international decisions. As Lester Korn, co-founder of the executive recruitment firm Korn Ferry, once declared, "Corporate leadership must now plan marketing strategies that are interrelated with the rest of the world. The CEO of the next five years must understand transnational strategies, new markets, and stronger competition."[4]

Business people in most manufacturing, natural resources, and services sectors will not have any choice but to globalize their operations, because the fastest growing markets will be in the developing countries. In fact, in the first four years of the 1990s, the leading industrial countries grew at an annual average rate of less than 2 percent, while the developing countries expanded at a rate close to 5 percent. As these countries continue to grow, so their production capabilities will become more sophisticated and their entrepreneurs, no longer satisfied with just their home markets, will seek to enter the economies of the G-7. In turn, competition in the advanced industrial countries will become more intense.

The firms that thrive will be those with internationally operating networks. They will be firms that are able to seize the growing range of opportunities that are coming to the fore. *World Investment Report 1993*, produced by UNCTAD, highlights the point in noting:

> The tendency for companies to put high-value functions in places where the best and lowest cost production capabilities exist is illustrated by the number of computer and software foreign affiliates (of multinational corporations) that are located in India, many of them in Bangalore.[5]

A decade ago it was unthinkable that an Indian city would become a highly competitive, global computer services center. But the unthinkable has happened, and this serves as a symbol of the Industrial Revolution. Today, in Bangalore, there is a concentration of engineers and scientists working in or around the city, all of whom are fluent in English. Bangalore's attractions are completed by its relatively low salaries, reflecting the abundance of labor and skills.

The time is ripe for companies of all sizes to capitalize on the immense opportunities in the Third World. This does not only apply to large corporations. Small- and medium-sized Japanese enterprises, for example, are leading the way in terms of going global outside of the ranks of the giant multinationals. They are investing heavily in the most advanced East Asian countries. They see their domestic production costs rising fast, and they recognize that if they are creative and flexible they can be in on the ground floor of the second Industrial Revolution.

However, tens of thousands of business people are still not aware that growth in other parts of the globe is now much more dynamic than in the advanced industrial countries. U.S. Secretary of Commerce Ron Brown noted in May 1994, after his first year in office:

> During my three trade and investment missions to Russia, the Middle East, and South Africa, nothing has so impressed me as the importance of directing American economic activities toward the world's emerging markets. Indeed, recognizing the value of these fast growing areas may be the biggest job of business in the 21st century.[6]

The 1980s and early 1990s in the United States, Japan, and Western Europe was a period of corporate reengineering and downsizing, a time of fierce competition and intense pressures by shareholders for greater returns on their investments. As we look to the future, however, upsizing will once again return, particularly for those who, in Brown's words, recognize the value of the emerging markets.[7]

Working in Informal Economies

To succeed, Western companies must invest in the developing countries and find new partners and joint venture opportunities. The rewards will be extraordinary for those who spend enough money and devote enough management time to this effort. Many of the most successful multinational corporations have already begun to move in

> **"To succeed, Western companies must find new partners and joint venture opportunities."**

this direction and have benefitted greatly from the new enterprises of the Third World as a result. The growth of increasingly more sophisticated domestic business environments in the emerging economies is another dynamic factor contributing to the overall boom scenario.

Across the Third World, a growing number of businessmen are becoming prominent, many of whom have evolved substantial, closely held family businesses far from public view. Much of their activity has been in so-called "informal," or "underground," economies, in which they overcome restrictions—and sometimes laws—to create enterprising opportunities. As these businessmen have prospered, they have sought to become part of the formal, or mainstream, economy and to participate on an increasing scale in international commerce.

To take just one example, the face of the new India can be seen in the dashing individuals who are coming onto the global scene there. They are worldly, urbane individuals, far removed from traditional concepts of Indian leaders. Nonetheless, they are well on their way to becoming billionaires. According to a recent *Forbes* article, included in this group are the Ruias brothers of Bombay, who have made their fortune in steel, shipping, construction, finance, oil, and gas; the Jindal family of New Delhi, who controls India's largest manufacturer of stainless steel; Pune Rahul Bajaj, worth at least $500 million, who owns the nation's largest motor-scooter manufacturing company; and the equally wealthy Goenka family of Bombay, who has huge interests in chemicals, pharmaceuticals, and information technology.[8]

In Latin America, in Africa, and across Asia, governments are putting policies in place that are enabling the informal economies to surface. People are being given tax and other incentives to, in effect, convert savings they have held in the informal economy into the formal economy—into government bonds and corporate equities and into commercial bank savings accounts. The flow of these resources into the mainstream, and the growing visibility in the formal economy of enterprises that have long been known to be larger than their official balance sheets might suggest, creates new momentum for Third World growth. It also provides multinational corporations expanded opportunities to find joint venture partners in the emerging nations and to tap local savings to complement their investment growth in these nations.

Recognizing Political and Economic Policy Changes

The mounting success of Third World countries to attract large flows of foreign direct and portfolio investment reflects the combination of hosts of specific social and economic policies, such as ones that bring the informal economy above ground. But all these policies are also moving ahead from a base of fundamental change in the attitudes of emerging nations towards multinational investment itself. This change is key to understanding the new era and being confident that the scale of investment flows is going to rise dramatically in coming decades. Increasingly, these governments have gained confidence, reduced protectionist barriers, and opened their markets to foreign trade and foreign investment. They have also created far more attractive political climates, drawing even more notice from multinational corporations.

In the last decade, we have seen economic liberalization and the spread of democratization across the globe. The song being sung most frequently by national leaders in the Third World today is capitalism; foreign multinationals, who 20 years ago were villified, are now being invited into these countries. The emergence of free market forces across the Third World as the central focus of policy makers has been replicated in the 1990s in Central and Eastern Europe. Now, for the first time in history, there is a universal acceptance of the notion of free enterprise and the rewarding of individuals for their entrepreneurial skills. It is difficult to overestimate the power this will have in pushing forward the global economy in the years to come.

Politicians, central banks, and national regulatory authorities in increasing numbers of developing countries are confident they can integrate foreign firms into the frameworks of their economic systems. They do not fear exploitation by foreign investors; rather, they believe that a fair partnership can be secured

> "For the first time ever, there is universal acceptance of the notion of free enterprise."

with such investors. They know they are in competition with other countries for the attention of foreign investors and must offer attractive investment packages—assurances on repatriation of earnings, tax concessions, work permit clearances, and so forth.

"I think that what is happening now will be looked on in retrospect as truly a new area of international political and economic thinking. And that is the acceptance of market-based principles around the world," says Arthur Zeikel, president and CEO of Merrill Lynch Asset Management. He adds:

> There is not a single, semi-industrialized country that is not embracing what used to be the American ideal of doing business and having a profit incentive, as well as reducing the involvement of government in business activities. These tendencies not only increase economic activity, but also economic and political freedom. What you have is a new world economy that requires investors to participate in this trend.[9]

The new Industrial Revolution will be exciting, but it will also be complicated. As Martin Sorrel has noted:

> I believe it will be increasingly important to do business internationally; I believe it will be increasingly fascinating to do business internationally. But I do not believe it will become any easier—it may indeed become more complex.[10]

3

Financing the New Infrastructure

usinesses which respond proactively to the second Industrial Revolution—those which adapt to policy changes
and learn to work with their partners—are the businesses
that will thrive in coming decades. But success takes
more than know-how and fortitude; it requires an enormous
capital investment as well, if a long-term, large-scale economic
boom is to be a reality.

Can the emerging economies raise the capital they need to ensure the essential mod-
ernization of their
economies? Yes. In
part, money will be
attracted to where the
growth is, and that
growth is going to be
in the emerging economies. Or, as Dean L. Buntrock, chairman of
the board and CEO of Waste Management, Inc., has noted, "Capital
is going to go where it can get the best return, and the best return
is going to come globally."[1] Indeed, it is already happening: Total
foreign direct investment in developing countries in 1993 hit an
all-time record of $80 billion.[2]

> "Succeeding in the coming boom will require enormous capital investment."

International investors are increasingly understanding that countries with sound economic policies and with pools of well-educated
individuals will attract major multinational firms of all kinds and
thereby strengthen the very base of their economic infrastructure.
Foreign firms also bring knowledge and management skills that

add strength to the overall infrastructural foundations of the newly industrializing economies.

The emerging economies that will be most successful in winning investments from the large multinational corporations and from the world's capital markets will be those which, above all, keep inflation low, maintain control of their balance of payments, ensure their economies are open to international investment and trade, and pursue sound and sustainable growth-oriented policies. Conversely, those nations with slack policies and controls will be dealt with harshly by the international community. The Mexican crisis in late 1994 and early 1995, for example, demonstrated to the governments of emerging economies that the price to be paid when governments become complacent will be large.

As noted throughout this book, a major funding source of new Third World business is foreign direct investment by IBM, Ford, Exxon, and growing armies of multinational corporations in brand new enterprises. International financial flows of money into equities and bonds from pension funds, mutual funds, and other institutions and rising numbers of individual portfolio investors are also playing significant roles in building the second Industrial Revolution. But these types of financial flows to the Third World will not suffice to secure the levels of economic growth that emerging nations both desire and can achieve.[3] In this chapter, we look at some of the other principal vehicles for attracting the necessary finance. These include privatizations, capital from expatriates overseas (notably the overseas Chinese and Indians), foreign aid, and domestic savings. First, however, let's continue our discussion of the great demand for money that exists—and is being met—in the emerging economies.

The Demand for Money

The scale of capital demands of the emerging economies is awesome. Current plans on the drawing boards of developing countries indicate at least $200 billion in infrastructure investments per year for the coming decade.[4] Non-Japanese Asia alone may well spend over $1 trillion on infrastructure investments in this period. Investments of power infrastructure investments alone in developing countries may be around $30 to $40 billion per year over the next decade.

Electric power systems are growing fast. Over the coming decade, for instance, South Korea intends to double its capacity from 20,000 to 40,000 megawatts, and the World Bank estimates that:

800,000 megawatts of new electricity generating capacity will be needed to satisfy global economic development in the next 10 years. This amounts to an investment requirement of $800 billion. Capturing even a small percentage of this market represents an enormous opportunity.[5]

Raising the funds for power investments will not be easy. However, Third World opportunities are revolutionizing the board rooms of once sleepy utilities in the U.S. and Europe. Management consultant George Hill has argued that a new perspective is emerging among utility companies, saying, "Utilities are breaking out of the traditional confines of their domestic markets by reinventing themselves to establish global operations."[6]

In addition to investments by the world's largest utility companies, the Third World's new power infrastructure is also receiving funds from many other sources of foreign finance. Major investors, such as the AIG insurance conglomerate, the powerful international investment funds directed by George Soros, and the General Electric Corporation, have also decided that the earnings in Third World power development are worth their investment.

The construction of new roads is another example of infrastructural advances for which Third World governments and their New York and London investment banking advisors are striving to find private financing approaches. In 1960, India had 254,446 km of paved roads; in 1990, that figure had nearly tripled, to 759,764 km. In the same period, the Philippines boosted its stock of paved roads from 6,356 km to 22,238 km, and Ecuador went from just 719 km of paved roads to 4,290 km. Each of these countries, however, will have to spend vast sums to establish road systems that match those in the most developed industrial countries.

Privatizations

As we alluded above, privatizations have been, and are going to be, a prime vehicle for emerging economies to attract the capital they need for modernization. The International Finance Corporation (IFC) has noted:

Recent years have seen a significant and continuing movement from state control of production facilities to private ownership. The privatization movement has targeted not only manufacturing plants but, even more important, activities ranging from financial services to infrastructure, including electricity, communications, transportation, and port facilities.[7]

It added that:

Between 1988 and 1992, governments in developing countries realized more than $60 billion in revenues from the sale of state-owned assets. Most privatizations have occurred in Latin America, but the trend is visible throughout the developing world: the Czech Republic, Hungary, Malaysia, Philippines, Poland, Portugal, and Thailand are just a few of the countries that have made significant progress in this area.[8]

Overseas Resident Capital

While many western investment banks and corporations have joined the Third World infrastructure financing game, that money alone is not enough. Vast amounts of money are also moving through unofficial channels among family interests so wealthy and influential that they represent extraordinary forces of economic influence in almost all less-developed countries. No group of this kind is more powerful than the overseas Chinese, mostly resident in Hong Kong, Taiwan, Singapore, Malaysia, Indonesia, and other nearby countries. The overseas Chinese will play lead roles in mobilizing the finances to secure the infrastructure developments now on the drawing boards, as will the powerful overseas Indians and many other wealthy indigenous Third World groups.

In an article in *Forbes* in July 1994, reporter Andrew Tanzer discussed the "bamboo network"—the sprawling diaspora of overseas Chinese who are pouring money into their homeland. There are an estimated 57 million overseas Chinese, overwhelmingly resident in Asia. Tanzer wrote that: "This vast, geographically dispersed community is accumulating wealth at a furious pace and generates an annual economic output of more than $500 billion (which by some estimates is rising by between 7 percent and 10 percent per year)."

In turn, the bamboo network shuttles its wealth back into China. An example is Dhanin Chearavanont, a second generation Thai of Chinese descent, estimated by *Forbes* to have a personal fortune upwards of $5 billion from telecommunications, food, manufacturing, and real estate businesses, who is investing hundreds of millions of dollars in China. He is not alone.

Tanzer pointed out that Malaysian Robert Kuok, known as "the Sugar King," has already committed $1 billion to investments in China, the country his shopkeeper and commodity trader father left early in this century. Another expatriate, Liem Sioe Liong, moved to Indonesia from Fujian, China, in the 1930s and today controls the Salim Group (Indonesia's largest conglomerate, with estimated annual sales of around $9 billion), which invests heavily in Fujian. And Li Ka-shing, who moved from Guangdong Province to Hong Kong in 1940, and who *Forbes* estimates has a net personal fortune of $5.8 billion, is said to be mobilizing billions of dollars of investments in Guangdong. Overall, the value of investments in mainland China by overseas Chinese exceeds $50 billion, roughly 80 percent of total foreign investment in China. They have also formed over 100,000 joint ventures in China.[9]

Numerically and economically, ethnic Chinese control Hong Kong, Taiwan, and Singapore, whose combined foreign reserves of $180 billion are equal to that of Japan and Germany together. In each country in Southeast Asia, the business holdings of the Chinese far exceed their ethnic representation in the population. For example, in Indonesia the resident Chinese account for no more than 4 percent of the population, but they own over 70 percent of private domestic capital and run more than 160 of the 200 largest businesses.

Tanzer stressed that culture, not politics, best explains the rise of overseas Chinese. They have displayed self-reliance and the Confucian virtues of thrift, discipline, industriousness, family cohesion, and reverence for education. Behind their dynamic economic success exists a vast web of interlinked, cooperative Chinese firms across Asia, all held together by verbal agreements and trust. And behind the web lies the family enterprise; it is the company that is the family and the family that is the company. Control of even the biggest firms resides firmly within the family.

Peter Berger, writing in the *McKinsey Quarterly*, added:

Clues to solving the riddle of East Asia's economic development are less to be found in Ancient texts—few Taiwanese entrepreneurs are steeped in the Confucian classics—or in time series data on key economic indicators (which simply reiterate what is already known), than in close, careful, ethnographically-oriented studies of the sort that anthropologists engage in when they endlessly interview and observe people in a culture they want to understand ... the approximately 50 million Chinese living outside mainland China who have played a disproportionately large role in driving the capitalist economies of their local societies ... Because the great majority of overseas Chinese firms are family owned, it is family culture that motivates the dedication, self-denial, sober pragmatism, cohesion, and flexibility of their employees. The explanation lies in the culture definition of trust. To the question, Whom can I trust? the Chinese answer is very clear—close relatives.[10]

In a microcosm, the importance of overseas Chinese comes fully into focus when looking at the relationship between Hong Kong and Guangdong Province to its north. Since China declared its "Open Door" policy in 1979, the scale of involvement by Hong Kong Chinese in the development of Guangdong has been massive and is a major reason why the Province's economy has grown by an annual average of over 12 percent. Between 1979 and 1992, Hong Kong accounted for almost 60 percent of the total foreign investment in Guangdong, compared to about 10 percent from Japan and 8 percent from the United States. Due to such heavy investment, Shenzhen, on the border between Hong Kong and Guangdong, has grown from a collection of villages in 1979 into a city three times as large as Hong Kong itself. And this is merely the tip of the iceberg of Hong Kong investment involvement in the development of China.[11]

Time and again, whether it be projects to develop suburban Beijing, the establishment of a banking system, or facilitating international trade growth, Hong Kong Chinese appear deeply involved. They are also helping to build vast numbers of individual entrepreneurs within China who can mobilize savings and develop investments on their own and in partnership with Hong Kong institutions and families.

The rapid rise of domestic entrepreneurs with world-class fortunes in developing countries is yet another major factor in determining whether the investment resources can be mobilized for essential infrastructure. These tycoons will enter into joint ventures with foreign entrepreneurs and make every effort to seize the new opportunities and put their money behind infrastructure investments that, within their economies, they believe can yield exceptional rates of return.

The number of these tycoons is expanding fast. While *Forbes* only looks at billionaires, its data is illustrative of the pace of change. The magazine's mid-1994 annual survey of the world's richest individuals noted:

> From the countries of the developing world—the emerging markets as they are now called—are springing individual fortunes in truly amazing numbers. In 1987, *Forbes'* first survey of world billionaires included only 6 Latin American billionaires, two of whom were cocaine lords, now dead; on this year's list there are 42 Latin billionaires, by all appearances every one of whom is legitimate. On the 1987 *Forbes* list there were only 14 Asian (non-Japanese) billionaires; in 1994 the number had grown to 146.

In addition to the overseas Chinese and Indians, the trends being set by Third World entrepreneurs in their own countries, multinational corporations, and investment banks are influencing increasing numbers of global corporate czars. *Business Week* reported in April 1994 that:

> Every time Daewoo Corp. (one of Korea's biggest industrial conglomerate enterprises) President Yoo Ki-Bum visits China, he can't resist making deals. In one of his six visits in 1993, the South Korean executive noticed that China had a lot of wood pulp, but not enough plants to turn it into paper. So he put together a quick joint-venture deal to produce high quality art paper in central China's Hubei Province. In the last two years, Daewoo Corp. has committed more than $400 million to investments in China. 'The opportunities are so vast,' says Yoo. 'I wish I had all the resources I needed.'

Foreign Aid

At one time, discussions of the capital requirements of developing countries started with reviews of foreign aid flows from the rich nations. Now only with regard to the very poorest countries of the world is this kind of decision still meaningful. Foreign aid

TOTAL NET RESOURCE FLOWS FROM OECD MEMBER COUNTRIES
(in billions of U.S. $)

	1985	1989	1993
Official Development Assistance (ODA)	44.1	61.1	66.6
Total export credits from governments	4.0	9.4	5.0
Total private flows	30.1	46.2	87.9
Combined total =	78.2	116.7	159.5
Breakdown of total private flows			
Direct investment	6.5	27.1	35.0
International bank lending	15.2	10.5	3.0
Total bond lending	4.2	1.3	36.6
Other private flows	1.3	3.3	7.0
Grants by nongovernmental organizations	2.9	4.0	6.3
Total private flows	30.1	46.2	87.9

remains important, and most emerging economies still need some forms of foreign official loans and credits, but aid now needs to be viewed as a supplement to private capital flows, not as the leading edge.

The data in the table above only reflects flows of funds from the 26 member countries of the OECD (the most advanced industrial countries). It shows that in 1985 ODA and export credits accounted for 61.5 percent of the total; the percentage was similar in 1989, but by 1993 the private sector had become dominant, accounting for 55.1 percent, and preliminary data for 1994 indicated an even higher share. Aid, in fact, is a small share of total capital flows to most developing countries. Almost half of all aid is provided by Japan, the U.S., and France (A great deal of the U.S. aid went to the Middle East, most Japanese aid went to Asia, and almost all French aid went to former French colonies in Africa). The probability is that, over time, overall ODA will decline, and, within the smaller volume, an increasing share will go to the very poorest and weakest economies.

Foreign aid budgets are being cut in most of the capitals of the West, and for the neediest nations this can spell disaster. But aid has become so small a percentage of the total capital now flowing to many emerging economies that, at least for the most dynamic emerging economies, the aid cuts are making barely any difference. In 1990, almost 50 percent of all flows of funds to the approximately 40 leading emerging economies came from foreign official creditors—by 1994 the level was down to around 10 percent.

A footnote on the role of official finance is in order: The economic recovery of many emerging economies from the debt crisis of the 1980s remains fragile, and, when poor policies surface, the well of foreign private capital can swiftly dry up. At such times, the availability of official foreign aid and loans can be a vital backstop—the multi-billion dollar Mexican bailout package from the West in early 1995 is a good illustration of this.

Domestic Savings

Another fundamental factor influencing the global capital markets will be the growth rates of the domestic markets of the developing countries. As they demonstrate the ability to sustain high levels, they will advance their international market credit ratings. As their ratings rise, so too will their ability to attract capital for infrastructure development. Perhaps as much as 80 percent of the total capital needs of the emerging countries will be supplied from the rapidly rising pool of domestic savings.

Generating the necessary savings demands the pursuit and implementation of sound economic policies by the developing countries, and more of them understand this today than ever before. New capital market structures are being put in place, better banking systems are being created, mortgage and insurance industries are evolving rapidly—indeed, in dozens of emerging economies the infrastructure is being built that can most efficiently mobilize savings. These domestic savings will be the magnets that attract foreign capital into partnerships. In turn, these partnerships will finance the infrastructure development boom that will power the new industrial revolution. In short, the boom will not fail for lack of money.

The combination of domestic and foreign money in financing the boom is only one facet of the multitude of linkages now bringing the economies of all nations more closely together. Energies are being unleashed in one corner of the globe that are spreading and stimulating growth in many other parts of the planet. There are now many poles of economic activity, and they tend to enthuse and support one another. The structure and sheer dynamism of this multipolar world is exciting.[12] It is also the critical base from which to understand the strength and breadth of the boom ahead, and the approaches that statesmen and business people must take to come to terms with this reality. In the next section, we will explore each of the poles that now comprise our global community.

4

China's Emergence as a Super Power

I n the past, when the United States economy caught a cold, the economies of the developing world caught pneumonia. No longer. We noted earlier that the emerging economies—especially those in Asia—have been growing steadily in recent years and have been able to do so even in times when Japan, North America, and Western Europe were in a slump. As we discussed, many emerging economies now have their own momentum and the capacity to contribute to world economic leadership. In short, we now live in a multipolar world, a world with numerous regions of economic viability, each with its own successes and failures. And each of these centers of economic activity is increasingly being integrated into the global economy and is adding to overall world economic growth. Now we will look at the dramatic events in different poles of this increasingly integrated global economy. Our aim is to highlight some of the fundamental trends and developments that are setting the stage for the coming boom. Our tour starts with China: the most populous nation on earth; the fastest growing large national economy in the world; currently, the magnet for more than one-third of all foreign direct investment flows to emerging economies.

China's Leadership

Asia holds the key to the coming boom. Philosopher Bertrand Russell predicted at the end of World War Two:

> I think if we are to feel at home in the world . . . we shall have to admit Asia to equality in our thoughts, not only politically, but culturally. What changes this will bring about I do not know, but I am convinced that they will be profound and of great importance.[1]

35

Travel to even the remotest regions of Asia underscores the scale and power of the economic advances taking place there. The traveler sees a transformation of life so vivid that, almost at a glance, there is a sudden understanding of the impulses about to be unleashed by hundreds of millions of peasants who obtain disposable income and begin spending on some luxuries of life. The following story is an example of what we mean.

The Runcai family lives in the Guanchuan River Basin area of Dingxi county in the province of Gansu. Few areas in all of western China are more barren. When Sacha Runcai was born in 1985, her parents lived in a crude mud and cement house, in conditions of extreme poverty. But in the late 1980s, the residents of this area—an army of over 90,000 farmers, including the Runcai family—used their bare hands and simple tools to reclaim hundreds of thousands of acres of land. Their work sculpted a vast terrain of terraced hills, maximizing natural irrigation possibilities and opening huge new cultivation prospects.

> "Asia holds the key to the coming boom."

As a result, the Runcai family now grows more food to sell in the markets. As they prospered, they were able to buy a tiny tractor, similar in size to a small U.S. lawn mower. It is a crude machine, with a lone exhaust pipe staring the driver in the face, yet it offers the Runcai family the passport to a new life. As their food output increased dramatically, they forsook their mud home for a new brick house. Within a handful of years, their lives have rushed from medieval times into the late 20th century.

Sacha and her parents now have a comfortable house, with stores containing large baskets of grain for the winter. They have electric power and their proudest possession in their neat living room is a 13-inch, black-and-white television set. It brings them foreign programs, Chinese educational shows, and commercials offering cosmetics, Western-style clothes, bicycles with gears, and other products of the modern world.

Just down the road from the Runcais live hundreds of people in rotten conditions. For them the present is as bleak as it ever was, but now they can see the future, not through television, but just by walking a few hundred paces to the tidy new homes that land reclamation and mobile farm machinery created. Life is changing for the people of Dingxi county.[2]

Deng Xiaoping's Vision

China's position as the leader of Asia in the new boom will change the way we all think about global relations. Former *New York Times* Beijing correspondent Nicholas Kristoff has noted that, while China is on a trajectory to displace the United States as the world's largest economy,"The international community is not giving adequate consideration to the colossal implications— economic, political, environmental, and even military—of the rise of a powerful China."[3]

Kristoff argued that we need to become used to the concept of a Greater China, comprised of China itself, Hong Kong, and Taiwan. On this basis, using World Bank projections, he stated:

> Greater China's new imports in 2002 will be $639 billion, compared to $521 billion for Japan. Likewise, using comparable international prices, Greater China in the year 2002 is projected to have a gross domestic product of $9.8 trillion, compared to $9.7 trillion for the United States. If those forecasts hold, in other words, Greater China would not be just another economic pole; it would be the biggest of them all.

China's leader, Deng Xiaoping, promoted free enterprise at home and strengthened support for the approach across the Third World. He turned a communist society that was chaotic following the Cultural Revolution into the fastest growing economy in the world. More than a dozen years ago, when only a few foreign firms took an interest in establishing ventures in China, Deng had articulated a vision for his country. In May 1983, he told visitors in the Great Hall of the People,"The most important objective of China is, by the end of this century, to shake off the shackles of poverty, and then we can contribute to the peace of mankind, and this is our most important priority."[4]

Deng said, by the end of the century, China, accounting for one-quarter of the world's population, could rise above its widespread poverty and become relatively well off. He continued:

> There is a story behind this. Two years ago, former Japanese Prime Minister Ohira came here, and he asked me what kind of society would we build here—what kind of modernization? And I really could not answer. We set our objectives for modernizations, but of what type? I thought for two minutes. I said we talk of the Chinese type of modernization, not the Japanese type, and we would not reach the type of modernization of the West. Then our per capita income was $250, and I said whether we can quadruple by the end of the century was our aim—$1,000 per capita is what I said to PM Ohira, and this is what I then saw as meaning relatively well off. We would make mistakes if we set an impossible target. We hope we can control population by the end of the century at 1.2 billion people, and, with so large a population, we might not reach $1,000 per capita. So, we reset our target to a more realistic $800 per capita, and this would mean a $1,000 billion gross output of industry and agriculture by the end of the century—this would be a large volume that we would consider as China's contribution to the world. And then moving into the next century in 30 to 50 years to build on what we have done in this century to make China a relatively developed country. For us, our target is a great ambition; others may think it minuscule.

William Overholt, managing director of Bankers Trust, Hong Kong, has pointed out that:

> China's strategy has created a vast class of new consumers who wear modern clothing and use modern amenities. Market research commissioned by Proctor & Gamble indicates that there are now tens of millions of Chinese who can afford five dollars to buy a bottle of Rejoice shampoo. China's Guangdong Province has become second only to the United States as a market for Proctor & Gamble shampoos. Avon has more than 18,000 Avon ladies successfully selling Western-style cosmetics door to door in Guangdong Province. Motorola, which rates China the best place in the world to manufacture electronic equipment, expects China to become its second-largest market in the world for second-generation cordless phones. All of this has revolutionized a society where only a decade ago a billion people dressed in the same shabby blue outfits and seemed to have had their hair cut with the same lawn mower."[5]

Barely a week goes by without a publication reporting a dramatic new set of statistics and investment stories concerning China. For example, *Chemical Week* has called China the chemical industry's "last fast-growing market."[6]
The magazine added:

> With the scale of opportunity for the chemical industry in China becoming clear, more foreign firms are lining up development plans. Traditionally, the chemical industry proceeded cautiously, but the past two years have seen the announcement of countless new projects, attracted both by demand opportunities and the efforts by local agencies and companies to attract foreign partners. The list of chemical companies that have announced plans is getting longer. For those that already have production ventures, projects are on a fairly modest scale; however, a new series of world-scale projects (involving investments of tens of millions of dollars) that will see China emerge as a global chemical industry player is nearing completion.

China's Realities

China's role in driving the new economic era is central, but can the political leadership in China continue the current policy course, which is leading to a more open society? Yes.

There is a reform momentum and a broad-based, spectacular rise in living standards in China that ensures that there can be no fundamental turning back from the present economic policy course. Political in-fighting at the top of the government is always possible and may slow economic growth for a time, just as spreading corruption may undermine real growth, but the free enterprise momentum of China is enormous. Between 1980 and 2000, the gross national product of China may very well double. Living standards have been rising fast, and the pace shows scant signs of slackening.[7]

Since 1978, China has pursued policies of reform in every part of its economy. Their widening acceptability is the explicit result of the unprecedented growth that they spawned. Critical policy changes have included:

- Farmers and nonagricultural enterprises now have greater freedom to determine the composition and pricing of output, to retain profits, and to decide on the disposition of retained earnings.

- Administrative decentralization has transferred more of the authority to plan and manage economic activity from the central government to provincial and local bodies, which are better informed about the local situation and are strongly motivated to promote development.

- Central control over the economy has been scaled back by reducing the number of commodities and the volume of production subject to mandatory plan targets and by decreasing the share of key products distributed through state-controlled channels.

- Although China remains an economy where public ownership is dominant, the government has permitted other forms of ownership (e.g., private, cooperative, foreign joint venture, etc.) and has supported these with the necessary regulations and constitutional amendments.

- Resources previously annexed by the state have been transferred to enterprises and rural producers, and this, together with a degree of fiscal decentralization, has given provincial authorities more discretion in taxation and expenditures.

- Product markets have been created, first in the rural areas and then extended to the urban sector, which allow producers to trade their above-plan output at freely determined prices.

- Financial reforms have dismantled the old monobanking system and increased the variety of financial institutions, as well as the volume and scope of financial transactions and instruments. The pronounced shift away from budgetary support of investment has reinforced the importance of the financial sector in mobilizing and allocating resources.

- Finally, external trade, now equivalent to over a quarter of gross domestic product, has opened up the economy significantly and, in parallel, a greater readiness to seek direct foreign investment in a range of manufacturing and service industries now exists. The creation of several Special Economic Zones, with adequate infrastructure, legislation governing foreign investment, and the steady elaboration of laws defining the rights of overseas businesses operating in China, have helped attract a large volume of foreign capital.

Given the mostly rural location of the population, the most crucial reforms from the perspective of modernizing China have come in the agricultural area. The success of these policies has been critical to China's growth and, thus, to the world's economy as a whole. Had agriculture stagnated, the efforts to create a more open economy would have floundered, and we would not be predicting a new Industrial Revolution now. But the policies were a tremendous success. For example, 50,000 communes were disbanded in the 1980s, and nearly 200 million family farms were reestablished.

Innovative programs have been launched in China to meet exceptional challenges to secure food supplies, build sufficient housing, modernize transportation, and ensure massive growth in energy supplies. But building a modern China, which is the most fundamental goal of the leadership, also demands securing increased foreign involvement in the economy to ensure technological innovation and rapid economic growth. China's leaders agree with this and are encouraging foreign commerce on an unprecedented scale. This is the prime reason for our optimism about China's outlook.

The excitement of foreign investors knows no bounds and adds to the picture of a rapidly strengthening Chinese economy. McDonald's, which has had its run-ins with the authorities in Beijing, is not atypical. Marvin Whaley, President of the company's China operations, spoke about the size of the market, stating, "In the U.S. there is one McDonald's for every 29,000 people. In Beijing, a city of 10 million people, there are just seven stores. In a city of similar size in the U.S., there would be 400."[8]

He added that the company has so far invested $50 million in China and opened 27 stores. It will double the number of stores in 1995 and again in 1996. By 2000, McDonald's aims to have 300 stores in China, with 600 in place by 2003!

Total employment in China has increased at an annual average rate of 2.9 percent, from 402 million in 1978 to 567 million in 1990. In the years ahead, the labor force will expand by approximately 16 million people each year (an amount almost equal to the total population of Australia). Ensuring productive employment for new labor force entrants and for the growing numbers of surplus farm laborers poses a major challenge to the economy—a challenge that has a direct effect on social stability. The further success of rural modernization is vital here, as is a growing volume of foreign, job-creating investment. As they continue to search for ways to employ their massive population, the Chinese will borrow large sums in international capital markets and offer many incentives to foreign firms to set up factories. These pressures make it certain that the next generation of Chinese leaders will not revert to the closed-society, conservative paths of the past.

China' s economy is growing rapidly, and the creation of a middle-class, where none existed before, is more visible and formidable here than in any other large, emerging economy. This new middle-class, with all its desires and new wealth, is a critical force in the growing and increasingly complicated network of trade and investment relationships between China and the rest of the world. It is a major source of strength for all of Asia' s emerging economies.

5

East and South Asia

ong Kong, Korea, Singapore, Taiwan, Malaysia, Indonesia, and Thailand are the "Tigers" of Asia. These countries are roaring ahead with an economic vitality that provides the firmest of foundations for the coming boom and serves as an inspiration for other emerging economies, such as China, India, and the poorer nations of East and South Asia.

Vast parts of the developing world have been transformed in recent years. Nowhere has this been more dramatically the case than among the Tigers. Here, and in China as well, absolute poverty (where people have barely enough food to survive) has fallen from one-third of the population in 1970 to one-tenth in 1990. In Indonesia, the proportion fell from 60 percent to 15 percent in this period; in China it fell from 33 percent to 10 percent; and in Malaysia and Korea today it is less than 5 percent. In fact, the number of absolute poor in East Asia is estimated to have fallen from 400 million in 1970 to 180 million in 1990. During the same period, the overall population grew by 425 million.[1]

Moreover, these countries increased their share of world exports from 5 percent in 1965 to 18 percent in 1990. Savings rates were lower than those in Latin America in 1965, but 20 percent higher on average by 1990. Between 1970 and 1989, real expenditures per pupil at the primary school level rose by 355 percent in Korea, while comparative expenditures rose by 64 percent in Mexico and 13 percent in Pakistan.

Lessons from the High Growth East Asian Countries

The Asian high performers, relative to other developing countries in the 1960–1990 period, achieved:

- More rapid output and productivity growth in agriculture.

43

- Higher rates of growth of manufactured exports.
- Earlier and steeper declines in fertility.
- Higher growth rates of physical capital, supported by higher rates of domestic savings.
- Higher initial levels and growth rates of human capital.
- Generally higher rates of productivity growth.

How did the Tigers achieve what has come to be known as the East Asian Miracle? The answer, according to World Bank research, is as follows:

> High rates of investment, exceeding 20 percent of gross domestic product on average between 1960 and 1990, including, in particular, unusually high rates of private investment, combined with high and rising level endowments of human capital, due to universal primary and secondary education, tell a large part of the story. These factors account for roughly two-thirds of the growth in these countries. The remainder is attributable to improved productivity.[2]

The East Asian Miracle is the product of many diverse factors coming together to ensure growth with widespread benefits. Strong institutions were established and directed by a high-quality civil service, consistent economic policies were pursued that created the appropriate environment for investment, education was a top priority, and the concept of shared wealth was strongly promoted to convince the broad public that benefits would result. For example, Korea and Taiwan carried out comprehensive land reform programs, Indonesia used rice and fertilizer price policies to boost rural incomes, Malaysia introduced programs to improve the lot of ethnic Malays relative to the better situated ethnic Chinese, and Hong Kong and Singapore undertook massive public housing programs.

The outlook for the East Asian countries is exceptional. They will lead the boom and serve as major magnets for foreign direct investment. These countries will create increasing numbers of very modern industries and challenge the most competitive corporations of North America, Western Europe, and Japan. They will join with the United States in demanding that the Japanese increasingly open their markets to imports, and this support will directly strengthen the U.S. diplomatic leverage in this crucial trade area.

In recent years the Philippines has lagged behind the progress of the Tigers, and its domestic political difficulties, combined with corruption, have undermined its potential. Now, the situation is changing. President Ramos appears to have created a base for real reform and progress. The major efforts being made, supported by the International Monetary Fund and, increasingly, foreign direct private investors, finally offer the prospect for the emergence of this country into the ranks of the fast-growing, emerging economies of the era of the new Industrial Revolution.

India

The economic success lessons of East Asia are now, at last, being absorbed by an increasing number of South Asian countries. India, with its population of 900 million people, is embarking on the most profound economic policy changes since it secured independence from British rule in 1947 and finally appears ready to become a major source of international growth.

India is a complex society. The visitor is stunned by the poverty—perhaps 200 million or more Indians live in conditions that are barely above survival levels. Our own experiences underscore the point.[3] To travel through Haryiana in northern India is to confront a time warp where a host of centuries jostle with each other in chaos. Modern cars, horns blaring, seek to progress through crowded towns, as camels saunter past, young men carrying all manner of baggage perilously weave in and out on noisy, cheap mopeds, and cyclists wind their way forward, oblivious to all around them—as oblivious as the women who walk erect down the sides of roads with large jugs of water balanced on their heads. A generation ago, the cars would have been a rarity; now, the camels seem out of place. A generation ago, the mopeds would have been remarkable; now, the women walking to the wells seem anachronistic.

A generation ago, the peasant farmer, when asked about his aspirations, would talk of his worries. He would have lamented that, after his death, his several sons would have to share the meager patch of land that he owns, and he would worry the land would not be able to support them and their families. Today, the farmer conveys a sense of hope. He talks of his sons working in modern factories or new shops in the nearby towns and of new, emerging markets, where he can sell more of his produce at better prices. Now, he talks of possibly buying a tractor and maybe even acquiring more land. He adds proudly that his neighbor has already become the owner of a television set.

The tempo of change in India is dramatic. The confusion that is created as modern industries rise, millions of people become middle class, and foreign investment emerges as a meaningful reality, is considerable. Sometimes the absurd illustrates the reality. For example, at Kodaikanal, in southern India, peasants assemble once a week at a central kiosk, where a television links them through a small satellite dish to their favorite program, "The Lifestyles of the Rich and Famous."

Along with the 200 million Indians who live in poverty, there are possibly another 40 million Indians who enjoy high living standards and another 150 million with significant disposable income. Within a decade, at current rates, it is estimated that this latter group of lower middle-class Indians could total more than 400 million people. In addition, there are several million Indians living outside of India (800,000 in the United States alone), many of whom have long waited for the day when governmental controls would be reduced, opportunities to invest in their home country would become available, and prospective returns on such investment would become reasonable.[4]

In the past, the civil service has run India. It has been concerned that an open, competitive society would lead to massive unemployment and social tensions that would smash the fragile arrangements that have secured democracy. In recent years, however, the government, led by Prime Minister Narasimha Rao, has introduced policies that seek to lift the yoke of an all-pervasive national bureaucracy from the backs of businessmen. In contrast to China, India has succeeded with political reform and liberalization long in advance of implementing efficient free market economic reforms.

Now, confidence in India's prospects as viewed by overseas Indians is rising and may lead to a new era of foreign direct investment that could create a momentum for growth similar to China's. Increasing numbers of the largest multinational enterprises are seeking opportunities in India and, as liberalization moves ahead, the opportunities will increase. Moreover, deregulation has given new life to the stock markets and, as the nation's capital markets open and become better regulated, they will attract increasing amounts of national savings.[5]

Like all developing countries, India has a substantial underground economy, and its beneficiaries, now seeing the dynamism of the formal economy, are finding the stock markets an effective means of getting their undeclared savings into the mainstream economy. The changes in economic management are yielding visible benefits across India and creating popular consumer backing for even greater reforms. There is now a momentum in India that provides Prime Minister Rao and other like-minded leaders with encouragement to proceed with deregulation. The civil service has no choice but to adjust to a new era.

The era of economic self-sufficiency is over. India has understood, albeit at long last, that the fortunes of its people will be best served by integrating its economy within the world economy to an increasing degree.

> **"The era of economic self-sufficiency is over."**

Many countries throughout the poorer parts of Asia are striving to replicate the Miracle. The combined contribution of the economies of South Asia to the global economy can be massive, if these countries can adopt the East Asian approaches.

Half of the world's extremely poor people, approximately 560 million, live in South Asia. The population total of India, Pakistan, Bangladesh, and Sri Lanka is close to China's total today, and, in the course of the next 30 years, it will grow at a faster rate than China's population. The Population Reference Bureau estimates that for the period 1990 to 2025, China's population will grow from 1.2 billion to 1.55 billion, while India's population alone will expand from 900 million to almost 1.4 billion.

Pakistan

In Pakistan, the key policy changes came in late 1991, with the election of an industrialist, Nawaz Sharif, as Prime Minister. In the following 18 months, Sharif rushed to launch privatization, sought

to liberalize and deregulate the economy, and introduced many of
the lessons derived from East Asia's success to Pakistan. Sharif was
an unskilled politician, however, and failed to control a volatile domestic political situation.

By mid-1993, the country was in a severe political crisis, and
there were fears that the military would again grab the reigns of
government. But, determined to build democracy and keep the public pledge for a full election in October, Pakistan's leadership searched
for someone of standing to be an interim Prime Minister. They found
Moeen Qureshi, then 62, just recovering from cancer and living in
Washington, D.C. Qureshi returned to the land of his youth for 14
weeks. His integrity and brilliance as an economist, coupled with
his lack of political ambitions, ensured that he was not a threat to
the established and entrenched political parties.

Qureshi did not waste time. He set new budget and monetary
policies, introduced economic liberalization and anti-corruption
measures, reached agreements with the IMF and World Bank in
record time, and set the stage for fair elections. Mrs. Benazir Bhutto
won the elections, and, while she has not supported all of Qureshi's
moves, she did not turn the clock back on the basic direction
of economic reform that Sharif had introduced and Qureshi
promoted.

Pakistan will adjust further, both because it needs foreign finance
to develop its infrastructure and because its rival, India, will set an
example for it to follow.

Growth Is Contagious

The momentum of India and Pakistan, if secured, will have a profound impact across South Asia. From Nepal and Sri Lanka to
Bangladesh, the urgency of economic reform is increasingly evident.
Many of the social, political, and economic problems must not be
underestimated, but, for the first time, an emerging middle class is
possible even here.

These examples are, in turn, having a profound impact on
countries that are only now beginning to join the global economy,
such as Vietnam, Laos, and Cambodia. These countries are seeking
to open their economies and follow the examples of others, and

they are already attracting the multinational corporations. The decision by President Clinton on July 11, 1995, to restore full diplomatic relations with Vietnam will strengthen the already substantial movement towards bringing this country fully into the global arena of trade and investment. Vietnam, as *The Economist* magazine declared on the cover of a special survey, is on "the road to capitalism."[7] Good policies, good governance, and free enterprise appear to be increasingly contagious.

Finally, an increasingly important participant in and beneficiary of these Asian economic developments is Australia. Industry here has rapidly become more multinational and much more focused on the Asian markets. The largest of all Australian enterprises, Broken Hill Propriety (BHP), is restructuring its organization to make it a far bigger force within Asia, and its example is being followed by other Australian enterprises. Asia, including Australia, is set for a long-term boom.

6

The Emerging Markets Beyond Asia

A sia's dynamism will be reinforced, and the global economy as a whole will be strengthened, by the growth in many other parts of the Third World. Nowhere is the drumbeat of economic activity and new entrepreneurship louder than in Latin America. Argentina and Chile, for example, were not so long ago ruled by corrupt generals and mired in debt. Now, they enjoy open democracies and rapidly developing modern economies. There are increasing signs of a new economic era elsewhere in the Third World, as well. Rarely before in modern times have there been better reasons for hoping that the economic potential of much of the Middle East, so long constrained by politics, might finally be realized. Much of sub-Saharan Africa is also making an unprecedented effort to attract foreign direct investment and to stimulate economic growth. Our purpose in this chapter is to elaborate on the points made in the opening three chapters by showing how the base is being put into place in many parts of the Third World, outside of Asia, to contribute to the long-term boom scenario that is now emerging.

> "After Asia, Latin America is the region most full of possibility."

After Asia, Latin America is the region most full of possibility. The strength of the U.S. economy, the boost to world growth initiated from the successes of the Asian economies, and the impulses created from the ratification of the North American Free Trade Agreement (NAFTA) combine to set Latin America on a long-term growth path. As the puzzle of the future world economic order is put together, there is every reason to believe the Latin pieces will be in prominent positions.

True to form, Latin America is marching ahead in zig-zag fashion. The long-term trend will be upwards, but as Mexico demonstrated in early 1994, there will be some inevitable troubles along the way. Most Latin countries will be increasingly strong magnets for direct foreign investment. It is probable that every one of the leading corporations in the United States will invest in that region in the next 10 to 15 years. In fact, the question is not if they will invest, but when, on what scale, and in which particular countries will they choose to invest.

For example, Latin America has already become almost a second home to Canadian mining companies. Policies from Peru to Guyana have been put into place to attract foreign mining houses to exploit the natural resources of the region. Chile, Peru, and Bolivia are enjoying a mining bonanza now—and this is just the tip of the foreign investment rush into a region of enormous economic potential.

The 1980s was the " lost decade" for Latin America. Social spending was slashed, poverty rose, and urban crime problems increased, as dozen of countries were forced to introduce austerity programs to deal with their huge foreign debts. Living standards fell for tens of millions of Latins. The debt crisis forced political reforms (ousting dictators and establishing democracies) and economic reforms that produced a leaner and more competitive economic base. Thus the 1990s, by contrast, is widely being hailed in the region as the "found decade." Numerous countries are starting to grow again, and they are structuring their advances in ways that make them efficient and competitive players in world markets.

Overall growth in the region by the mid-1990s was on an upward trend from 2.9 percent in 1992 and 3.3 percent in 1993. Of the seven leading countries that together account for over 95 percent of the region' s economy, only Venezuela and Mexico had sluggish growth in 1993 and 1994. Inflation in most countries was moderating, and the overall external balance of payments was showing signs of improved health. Here again, however, Mexico was an important exception.

The debt crisis forced leaders in the region to face realities. For one, they could no longer endlessly turn to foreign banks for funds for their reckless national management. They now needed to enact budgets that matched national capacities. This not only demanded that bloated bureaucracies be deflated and welfare programs be reviewed, it also meant recognizing that most state enterprises were inefficient drains on scarce national finances. Privatization became an essential component of policy; it could reduce budget deficits by curbing government subsidies and by attracting foreign payments for domestic assets.

Latin governments also recognized that the inefficiencies of their economies were partly due to protectionist policies and excessive state regulation of the economy, both of which served to quash competition and encourage corruption and waste. Liberalization, deregulation, and privatization became the orders of the day and the bases for confidence in the future. These political and economic changes are attracting increased numbers of foreign, long-term, investors.

The modern economic structures and policies that are evolving in Latin America can create a new Industrial Revolution here almost as boldly as in Asia. Similarly, the leading edge of the investment in future growth is from the substantial pools of domestic savings, increasingly augmented by foreign investment. The fruit of the new investments will take some years to blossom, but by the late 1990s, the base for major, long-term growth will be firmly established.

The scale of foreign direct investment into the region by major U.S. corporations highlights this fundamental optimism. News reports, each and every day, of new investments into Latin America compete increasingly with those that emerge from Asia. Latin America could well double its annual level of economic growth in the years ahead. It has the potential, and it may, in time, have the political leadership.[1]

Middle Eastern Prospects

The Middle East and Mediterranean region represent another pole of economic activity, linked to all the others, that is both benefiting from, and contributing to, the dynamism of the whole. The picture is a mixed one in this area, which stretches from Iran and Turkey through the Middle East to North Africa. Political pressures throughout the region are intense and have been a major distraction from sound economic management, although some countries, namely Turkey and Egypt, are striving for economic success.

A bullish factor of note is the possibility of peace between the Arab states and Israel. The recognition of Israel by Saudi Arabia, combined with historic developments with regard to the Palestinians, provides an opportunity to divert large resources, currently devoted to arms, to peaceful, economic purposes. Indeed, peace can create levels of economic activity that have not been seen in this region in modern times.

Many of the region's countries will be affected by the oil outlook. The boom in much of the world will unleash demand pressures on supplies of raw materials. It will be some years before a new infrastructure is in place that enables developing countries to use energy efficiently. For the remainder of this decade, barring a slump in the industrial countries that would curb overall international petroleum demand, an upswing in oil prices is probable, and it may have a modestly negative impact on overall economic growth.

Moreover, in the mid-1990s, several of the most important oil-producing countries, including Saudi Arabia, were confronting cash-flow problems. These may be relieved by the rising Third World demands for petroleum to fuel rapidly growing economies. Such relief would secure continuation of developments in the Middle East and parts of North Africa, thus strengthening the region's entire economy.

This good news must be tempered by the broad threat of Islamic fundamentalism, stretching from Iran into Turkey and Central Asia, across to Algeria, and elsewhere in North Africa. It is difficult to forecast what will happen on this front, or what the outlook for the region will be, so long as Iraq remains a dangerous enemy to virtually all of the countries on its borders. One of the biggest fears pertains to the reliability of oil flows from the Middle East to fuel the new Industrial Revolution.

In spite of the possible spread of fundamentalism, the region has the potential to be part of the multipolar system, strengthening its economic linkages to all other regions and thereby strengthening both its own prospects and those of the global economy as a whole.

Africa's Huge Challenges

Our perspective is equally muted with regard to most of the countries of sub-Saharan Africa. In fact, there is a danger that the new Industrial Revolution will simply bypass much of Africa. Many African countries must still prove that they can secure stable governmental systems, and many others have yet to demonstrate their capacity to manage the ever-increasing number of social and economic problems with which they are faced. From 1990 to 2025, the population of sub-Saharan Africa is set to rise from 500 million people to 1.3 billion. Poverty is rising, AIDS is spreading, drought remains a problem in numerous areas, and environmental erosion is moving ahead at a rapid pace.

South Africa may have a major influence on changing things for the better in much of the region. Nelson Mandela took the oath of office as President of South Africa on May 10, 1994, declaring that "Out of the experience of an extraordinary human disaster that lasted for too long must be born a society of which all humanity will be proud." [2] Mandela grabbed the imagination of the world and the attention of his people and launched a new era for his country, an era equally full of promise and danger. He took over a country whose white elite had accepted him only with the greatest of reluctance—and then only after having put him in prison for twenty-seven years. Apartheid did not end because the whites desired a multiracial country; it ended because they had no alternative.

By the start of the 1980s, it was obvious that time was running out for the white leadership. The business and government communities of South Africa were corrupt. They conspired to enrich themselves by exploiting the black majority population. But the mass was getting larger, as was the number of unemployed youth. South Africa needed huge new foreign investment, without which there would be no means to establish new jobs, but the U.S., in particular, was leading a business boycott of South Africa, so new investments were scarce. The African National Congress and others outside of the country were also proving effective in sustaining the boycott, and the white leadership confronted an ever-growing danger of social instability.

Although President Frederik de Klerk had no desire to share power, let alone see his country have a black president, by the mid-1980s, he understood that the alternative could be a terrible bloodbath. From that point onward, he concentrated his efforts on the goal of ensuring that the bloodbath would not happen. He succeeded, primarily because he found in Mandela a man of vision and reason who possessed the charisma to secure a peaceful transition.

The challenge now is for the good start to lead to a new economic dynamism. This demands a fresh, transparent relationship between government and business, and full accountability by elected politicians to all of South Africa's citizens. The simultaneous transformation of the economy and the political system is as daunting for South Africa as the challenge that confronts Russia. Those who have taken high political office and leading civil service positions have no government experience and very little knowledge of business.

If its new leaders can succeed, South Africa can not only become a full participant in the new Industrial Revolution, deriving enormous benefits from demands for its products from developed nations and from Asia, but it can also provide intense energy to assist the countries to its north.[3] The Southern African Development Community, consisting of 11 countries, can become a dynamic region if there is a strong South Africa, but without it their prospects are bleak.

Botswana, Zambia, Namibia, Zimbabwe, Tanzania, Angola, Mozambique, Malawi, Lesotho, and Mauritius, for example, all need foreign investment, and South Africans are the most obvious investors here. With this inflow of cash, their natural resources can be fully utilized, providing immense benefits to the peoples of these poor nations. South African investment leadership can also attract significant investment from Europe and North America, and bring with it the vital technological and managerial skills that these countries need.

> **"The success or failure of most African countries will depend on their domestic policies."**

But South Africa cannot do it on its own. The success or failure of most African countries to prosper from the economic boom ahead will depend on their domestic policies. If they cannot curb corruption and secure political systems that enable economies to flourish, then their peoples are doomed to further desperate hardship. As Botswana, Namibia, and Ghana have shown, for example, foreign official aid and foreign direct investment are both available to African countries that pursue sound economic policies of reform and adjustment, much in line with the East Asian model, within environments of political stability. There are also a number of countries, such as Tanzania and Uganda, that are somewhat less developed, but which are moving firmly in the right economic policy direction.

The Metals Bonanza

While the major natural resources companies are taking close looks at Russia, they recognize the political risks there are particularly great. As a result, the new exploration and development programs are for the most part being focused on Latin America, parts of Asia, and, increasingly, on Africa. For example, 200 representatives of the North American mining industry converged on Denver in mid-1994 for a unique set of presentations by 16 African mining ministers on the investment opportunities in their countries. A decade earlier it would have been impossible to attract much interest in a conference like this. The conference was also extraordinary in that so many African leaders went to such lengths to underscore the interest of their nations in attracting foreign private investors. Numerous African countries could enjoy a bonanza, due to their vast natural resources and to the Industrial Revolution in Asia. The prime beneficiaries may be the countries in Eastern and Southern Africa, notably Uganda, Tanzania, Mozambique, Zimbabwe, Botswana, Zambia, and South Africa.

African metals supply will be crucial as Asian metals demands rise, as a result of infrastructure construction and the vast needs of the rising consumer class in Asia. The countries of Eastern and Southern Africa have the opportunity, if they can seize it, to maximize their logistical advantages in being able to ship metals to rapidly growing Asia and in competing because of their very low production costs.

continued

The Metals Bonanza (concluded)

Nickel, for example, will be a prime beneficiary of this new Asian demand, and very substantial nickel deposits exist in Tanzania. As a result of the boom already emerging, nickel could trade at more than double the average price seen in 1994, $7.50 per pound, as early as from mid-1996 to the year 2000, and then go still higher. Cobalt may be another exceptional metal to benefit from this scenario. Again, the production prospects in Africa are substantial. The price of cobalt could also double in the same time horizon and move to around $50 per pound.

And the gold picture is also a bullish one. Africa has enormous, untapped gold wealth. The world' s leading mining companies are now moving at speed to Ghana, Mali, and other west African countries, and to Tanzania and Zimbabwe in the East, to explore for gold. They are being welcomed by governments that want foreign direct investment. They see the Asian demand prospects.

The greatest demand for African gold will come first from China and then India. The new middle classes here will, for at least another generation, display no trust in paper currency. They will see gold as a storehouse of value. Gold jewelry will be in strong demand as a form of currency in Asia, and much of the supply will come from African mines through the Middle East, with leading mining companies also supplying direct. In the immediate years ahead, the gold price could easily trade in a range of $350 to $525 per ounce.

Africa is no monolith. The political conditions prevailing in Nigeria, which accounts for one-quarter of sub-Saharan Africa' s population, are chaotic and getting worse, and corruption is the prime disruptive force. By contrast, we have found from our own experiences that a genuine, open, multiparty democracy is providing meaningful strength to Tanzania, right across the continent from Nigeria. Africa will remain a continent of contrasts. Because of political instabilities, its vast mineral treasurers will largely remain far from exploitation for many years to come. But there will be countries to emerge from this part of the world whose economic future will blossom, whose mineral riches, combined with excellent transportation prospects, and sound political conditions, will combine to yield positive results.

While increasing numbers of investors are looking to Africa' s resources—from all kinds of metals to oil and natural gas—we still question whether most African countries will be able to join the ranks of emerging markets. In all probability, some countries will do quite well providing the rest of the world with essential raw materials. However, many African countries may continue squandering their assets and dive to still lower living standards and graver political problems. These latter countries may continue to be the focus of the Western media, but the success stories should not be overlooked.

As a landmark study by the United Nations concluded in mid-1995:

> One of the messages from our analysis is that Africa is a continent in which profitable investment opportunities do exist, and that transnational corporations should consider African countries as investment locations.[4]

The fact is, in Africa, just as in the Middle East, numerous countries will prove able to add vitality to the world economy. They will strengthen the boom and hasten the spreading of the new Industrial Revolution. To disregard these regions is cynical and unwise.

The key to prosperity today in many of the countries of Africa, the Middle East, and Latin America is politics. The adoption of free enterprise approaches in the last dozen years, particularly in the first half of the 1990s, has coincided with new forms of political openness. There is more of a free press in Africa today, for example, than ever before. There are more mass movements publicly calling for the end of corrupt government practices in Latin America than ever before. Progress on the political and economic fronts is being realized, and it is leading to the establishment of a new middle class in many of these countries. The development in these countries, coinciding with similar advances in China and the rest of Asia, is creating the new Industrial Revolution.

7
East and West— Poles Apart

I f substantial economic growth can be secured in Central and Eastern Europe and in the leading Western industrial countries while the new Industrial Revolution unfolds in the Third World, then the combined impact will be phenomenal. We are not certain that this will be the case, and we are acutely aware that, in outlining our boom scenario, we need to address two popular and important questions:

- Can free enterprise really succeed in the former communist countries of Central and Eastern Europe ?
- Can our lifestyle in the West be sustained as new Third World industries emerge with competitive furor to challenge the major corporations of North America, Japan, and Western Europe ?

The search for answers to these questions has been the substance of many articles and books in recent years. There will continue to be optimists and pessimists galore to argue the details. Our purpose here is not to stir the controversies, but to outline some of the realities and note our own conclusions. We will start by looking at the prospects for Central and Eastern Europe and then the challenges that face the West.

Central and Eastern Europe

Can Central and Eastern Europe reshape its political and economic landscape to take fullest advantage of its immense natural resources, significant physical infrastructure base, and the high educational

standards of its people? If it can, then this pole of the global economy can contribute formidably to the boom ahead. But, we are far
from certain. We want to take a positive approach, yet we daily see
abundant situations to give us pause.

Jacques de Larosière, the eloquent president of the European
Bank for Reconstruction and Development (EBRD), noted in a speech
in Moscow in mid-1995 that Russia faced the central structural problems of an inefficient and corrupt tax system, an uncertain legal
framework governing business, and a poorly regulated securities
market. It is precisely these factors that have worried us the most
and prompted us to reach the same conclusion as Mr. de Larosière,

> At present, there appear to be two alternatives: On the one hand,
> Russia could become a distorted market economy, centered on a
> limited group of lobbies vying for a slice of the stagnant pie...or
> Russia could become a transparent, rule-based market economy.[1]

In spite of seventy years of communism, the historical relationship
between Russia and many of its neighbors is just as tenuous as
ever, if not more so. The Soviet Union was never the federal system
of equal republics it purported to be; instead, it was always an empire dominated by Russians. The communist leadership in the Kremlin may have replaced the czars, but the approach was the same: to
exploit the wealth of many parts of the empire for the benefit of
Russia. When the Soviet Union broke apart, each of the republics—
from Belarus to Uzbekistan—hoped to attain independence from
Russia. The Russian leadership, however, never cast aside its belief
that Russia was superior to its neighbors and had a right to continue to seek to control them or much of their affairs.

The tensions between Russia and the former states of the Soviet
Union are high. The cultures of many of these states—from the languages spoken to the religions that dominate the lives of many of
their citizens—are different. The determination to be free of Moscow's
shackles has been a driving force behind much of the fervent na-
tionalism seen in a large part of the region. In Armenia, Georgia,
and Azerbaijan, as well as in Russia itself—boldly demonstrated, by
the uprising in Chechnya—bitter internal conflicts have erupted
as different factions seek the nationalist leadership of their countries. As these states seek their independence from Moscow, so the
weakness of modern Russia is itself a theme within the country,

exploited by populist leaders like Vladimir Zhirinovsky, an extreme rightwing politician who has sought to exploit the weakness of President Boris Yeltsin.

The first priority for the political and military leaders of the region is to establish secure, independent states and a coherent sense of national identity. Given the many ethnic and other divisions in several of these states, not to mention the acute declines in output and living standards in recent years (starting well before the collapse of communism), it is difficult to determine just when these political goals will be accomplished. In the meantime, until there is a considerably improved sense of political stability, it is difficult to see how coherent, tough, long-term programs of economic policy adjustment are likely to be sustained, or how effective rules of law that create more stable economic conditions and institutions can be firmly established.

In the first four years of the 1990s, industrial production in Russia halved. The pace of decline had slowed by late 1994, as had the tempo of inflation, and there were increasing numbers of media reports of the sun starting to rise—optimism showing through, as Russians started to eat more meat and chicken and shortages diminished. The OECD reported that there may have been some real stabilization of the economy in the first quarter of 1995, and that growth may at last emerge in 1996.[2] Moreover, it is likely that the Russian underground economy may be close to the same size as the official economy, meaning that living standards may be twice as high as official statistics suggest. All the same, the national budget deficit is soaring and the scale of debts that major companies owe each other is reaching fantastic proportions. Also, corruption and crime are widespread, because of the lack of effective social safety nets for the poor and the newly unemployed in a society where unemployment is rising rapidly.

The biggest worry is that these problems will not be managed by mid-1996, the date of the next presidential election, where the contest may be between the advocates of economic transformation to a liberal, free market system and the advocates of staunchly conservative, authoritarian government. From the West's perspective, the danger of radical nationalists taking power in the world's second and third most powerful nuclear nations, Russia and the Ukraine, is a concern.

Looking at Central and Eastern Europe demands recognizing that China and other Asian nations have demonstrated that economic reform and restructuring may best be secured in underdeveloped countries within a highly regulated political system, and that relaxing the system, which is an inevitable demand from increasingly affluent populations, may have to be a gradual process to ensure stability. The overthrow of communism was a public protest about a political system, not a vote in favor of American and West European free enterprise. There is no evidence to suggest that most Russian people had any notion of what free enterprise, profit, and individual incentive were all about.

The West may have mistakenly urged the new post-communist leaders to move too fast on the economic reform front; a slower pace, allowing for greater consolidation and strengthening of new democratic political institutions, might have been far wiser. Alternatively, perhaps the West, seeing the opportunities that the collapse of communism provided, should have ensured effective economic transformation by launching a huge financial assistance program—in effect, a new Marshall Plan—running into tens of billions of dollars. The West did not do this; instead, it provided relatively modest sums and, in the case of loans to Moscow from the International Monetary Fund, moderate sums with major economic policy conditions attached.

Clouding the outlook even more is the military, which waits in the wings in Russia, and elsewhere in this region, in the event that the experiment with democracy and economic liberalization fails. William Overholt has argued with regard to Russia:

> The notion that one can have all good things (democracy and all forms of economic liberalization) instantly and simultaneously has proved to be an ideological assumption in the strictest sense: a deeply held belief that has no grounding in practical historical experience. In this case, we Westerners are, in fact, caricaturing our own ideology: There is an explicit set of assumptions—such as efficient information flows—in capitalist economics, which clearly depend on institutional structures that have not been present in Eastern Europe and take time to build. Likewise, there is a literature on prerequisites of democracy that dates back to the Greeks, and few of these prerequisites are satisfied by countries in the Third World or Eastern Europe. One cannot build a modern glass-and-steel skyscraper just by putting dynamite under an old brick building. Trying to create

modern market democracies just by blowing up old socialist structures is equally futile.[3]

The successful Asian countries demonstrate the vital need for strong institutions to support economic development; these are absent in Russia and in the former Soviet Union. As a result, many foreign investors are incurring great frustrations as they enter these markets. For example, as *Forbes* reported in August, 1994, Phibro Energy, a subsidiary of Salomon Inc., which had started investing in the energy sector in Russia in 1990, thought of quitting because the constant changes in Russian law and administration created havoc with the company's plans. In one incident, the government annulled a guarantee that Phibro could export oil free of Russian export taxes, and in its place the government imposed taxes that equal almost 70 percent of Phibro's gross revenues. In another example, Gulf Canada cut off all further investment in a Russian oil field where it had already committed $60 million, because taxes on Gulf's venture would exceed 100 percent of total revenues.

While the foreign companies are getting hit, all sorts of domestic entities appear to have won special privileges, providing them with advantages over foreign firms seeking to invest. As former Russian Finance Minister Boris Fyodorov said in 1994, "It's a replay of the last days of Gorbachev, with the leader talking about reform while giving favors and privileges to the groups who most strongly oppose it."[4]

If there is one surprise on the Russian reform front, it is the pace of mass privatization. Thousands of enterprises have been moved from the government's ownership and control to the private sector. As much as 40 percent of the nation's output is now in the private sector. But, even here there needs to be a word of caution. For example, economists at the OECD warned:

> The tendency in Russia to create groupings of banks and already privatized enterprises may well concentrate ownership and financial resources and risk, resulting in control by closed rent-seeking groups, rather than the installation of outward-looking, efficiency-seeking management—it may also undermine the independent development of the financial sector.[5]

In most Central and Eastern European countries (Hungary, the Czech Republic, Slovakia, Slovenia, and Poland are the exceptions) there is no tradition of free enterprise, independent civil service, or democracy in any form. Tremendous education is needed to build public understanding of how capitalism works and how such institutions as an independent judiciary, meaningful private property rights, shareholder responsibilities and rights within private corporations, and a free press are imperative if far-reaching political and economic reforms are to work.

In the current environment, where Western hopes are so high that the transformation in the region will succeed, there is a constant tendency for Western politicians and business people to grasp at straws, magnify the successes, and make positive claims that overstate the realities. And the handful of countries that are moving toward real economic growth and putting modern structures in place are being hailed as brilliant success stories—sometimes greatly understating the remaining major political and economic problems that exist. This is as true of Poland, for example, and of Hungary.

> **"There is a desperate need for foreign advanced technologies, managerial skills, and Western capital."**

At a minimum, it may be several years before foreign private business confidence in the former Soviet Union area reaches levels that lead to substantial flows of investment resources, but such resources are crucial to modernizing and restructuring the economy of this region. There is a desperate need for foreign advanced technologies, managerial skills, and Western capital. Without these, the economic prospects in many parts of the region are not good.

To be sure, some of the countries in the region have started to record positive economic growth, most particularly the Czech Republic (which has already transferred 80 percent of national production into the private sector through the most successful privatization program in Central and Eastern Europe), Poland, the Slovak Republic, and Slovenia. These countries have been able to adapt with sufficient speed to take advantage, in the last couple of years, of the improving growth situation of West European economies and their growing demand for goods and services from the East. The OECD asserts about East-West trade that, "It can be expected that linkages will become even more pronounced, as both trade barriers and mutual ignorance of available trade opportunities continue to be reduced."[6]

The new Industrial Revolution offers an exceptional opportunity to assist the transformation of the former Soviet Union. China and much of Asia will have outstanding demands for natural resources that Russia and the Central Asian republics can supply. The growth of the Western European economies provides market opportunities for all manner of exports from Central and Eastern Europe. Thus, the opportunities will be abundant. But can the political organization be put in place to take full advantage of this potential?

To a point, we are skeptical. In Romania and Bulgaria, to take just a couple of examples, the old communist guard is back in power and large privatizations are, in effect, merely the transfer of ownership and control of enter-

> "Emerging nations are forcing business in North America, Japan, and Western Europe to be more competitive."

prises from the official public sector to private individuals who are either in the political leadership or are associated with it. Corruption, as we note in Chapter Nine, is pervasive in the region.

We do not believe that politics in this region will become so radical as to undermine world stability and wreck hopes of a new era of world prosperity. Indeed, it is this very threat that is the central preoccupation of Western foreign policy leaders and the impulse behind efforts to broaden the scope of NATO and create new relationships between East and West. Nor do we believe, however, that changes will be quick and easy. If we are proven to be too pessimistic, then we shall be delighted, because the success of the region will unquestionably contribute to global peace and security and provide still greater energy to the global boom predicted in this book.

Challenges to the West

Some industries in the West view the emerging economies of the new Industrial Revolution as threats, increasingly competitive, and likely to create Western unemployment. In fact, we believe that just the opposite is true: The emerging nations are actually forcing businesses in North America, Japan, and Western Europe to be wiser, more creative, and more flexible. Rather than view the emerging economies as threats, we should view them as positive challenges.

With these new challenges before us, however, Western nations can no longer rest on their laurels. They will only stay ahead by finding smarter ways to produce, earning more of their profits in the Third World, and building the first international economic super-highways to integrate the global economy on an unprecedented scale.

OUTLOOK FOR INDUSTRIAL COUNTRIES THROUGH 1999
(annual percentage changes in real economic growth)

	1994	1995	1996–99
All Industrial Countries	2.7	2.7	3.0
United States	3.7	2.5	2.4
Japan	0.9	2.5	4.1
Germany	2.3	2.8	3.1
France	1.9	3.0	2.9
Italy	1.5	2.8	3.4
United Kingdom	3.3	3.0	3.0

Source: *IMF Medium-Term Outlook*, published in September 1994.

Rarely has the general environment for such developments been as positive as it is now. As the table above indicates, the economic growth outlook for the top industrial countries to the end of this decade is good. The International Monetary Fund is predicting the kind of business climate that can support precisely the innovation necessary to ensure that the West adapts to the realities of an emerging Industrial Revolution in the Third World.[7]

The West has been telling the Third World for decades, and the governments of Eastern Europe in more recent times, that their path to prosperity lies in the pursuit of open trade and investment. Free trade produces healthy competition. What we need to realize now is that this is as true for the West as it is for the less-developed nations. Indeed, while U.S. trade unions place the blame for rising unemployment rates on free trade agreements, the fact is that western consumers will see their living standards shrink if high tariff walls are created to prevent the import of goods and services from the emerging economies. This, in turn, will reduce domestic demands, factories will close at home, and unemployment will grow.

It is no accident that the fastest rise in living standards in the history of the world was seen in Canada, the United States, Japan, and Western Europe between 1950 and 1970, a period coincident with the most rapid liberalization of international commerce in history. The tariff walls started to crumble, the protectionist barriers started to be dismantled, and the world prospered. The boom in the emerging economies is unleashing similar competitive pressures, and the adjustments in the Western economies are difficult and painful; we do not mean to minimize this strain. However, if we recognize the pressures and adapt to a world of more competition, then we will benefit.

> "The reengineering of IBM, GE, Xerox, and Kodak are a positivie step in preparation of the coming boom."

For the most part, Western countries (led by the United States) will adapt and contribute substantially to the full scale and breadth of the new Industrial Revolution. The ratification of a new world trade liberalization treaty at the end of 1994 was a crucial test. The decision in the U.S. Congress, and in other legislatures in the advanced industrial countries, to vote for free trade was a rejection of the protectionists and a building block for a brighter global economy. So, too, is the extensive reengineering of corporations like IBM, GE, Xerox, and Kodak as part of the massive adaptation to a more competitive business world that will be positive for the American and global economies.

Most countries will adapt, because their leaders recognize that they have no choice. The single greatest force for structural adjustment and far-reaching policy change in most industrial countries is unemployment. As illustrated in the table below, the OECD reported in 1994 that there were 35 million people unemployed in OECD countries. Perhaps another 15 million have either given up looking for jobs or have unwillingly accepted part-time jobs and, in some countries, as many as one-third of young workers have no work. To put these figures in perspective, during the 1950s and 1960s the total number of unemployed in OECD countries averaged below 10 million, but within just one decade, from 1972 to 1982, this number tripled. The economic expansion of the 1980s reduced the unemployment total to 25 million, but the level has been on the rise again since 1990. The most serious long-term unemployment difficulties have been experienced in Europe.[8]

UNEMPLOYMENT LEVELS IN LEADING INDUSTRIAL COUNTRIES
UNEMPLOYMENT RATE (1993) AS A PERCENTAGE OF THE
TOTAL LABOR FORCE

	Long-Term Unemployed All Persons	Youths	Women	Jobless
United States	6.7	13.3	6.5	11.2
Canada	11.1	17.8	10.6	11.2
Japan	2.5	5.1	2.6	15.4
Germany	5.8	4.9	6.1	33.5
France	11.6	24.6	13.7	36.1
Italy	10.2	30.6	14.6	58.2
United Kingdom	10.3	16.9	8.1	35.4

Unemployment rates for youths and women refer to 1992. The long-term jobless rate is a share of total 1992 unemployment in percent and is defined as persons without jobs continuously for one year or more.

Source: OECD.

In a landmark study of Western unemployment, the economists at the OECD in Paris found that technology has created jobs, not joblessness. They found:

The single most important cause of rising unemployment, as well as a growing incidence of low-wage jobs, is a growing gap between the need for OECD economies to adapt and to innovate and their capacity, and even their will, to do so.

The emerging economies have demonstrated great skill in adapting to changes and to evolving their economies in line with new, international pressures and realities. The leading developed countries, in contrast, have found adaptation harder, but an increasingly integrated and competitive world provides decreasing opportunity to avoid the tough choices. A multipolar, swift moving, global economy demands, according to the OECD researchers, that Western governments and businesses promote growth-oriented policies, strengthen the environment for research and development and skills training, encourage work-time flexibility, review minimum wage laws, boost the entrepreneurial climate, and reform unemployment benefits and related benefit systems to encourage people to work.

The United States, Japan, and Germany are already well advanced in adopting many of these policies. Their example is likely to be followed by most of the other developed industrial economies. If they succeed, then the period ahead could see new vigor in many of these economies. The underlying fundamentals for this are already largely in place.

Critical Roles for Free Trade

The multitude of poles of economic activity forces increasing pressures in international relations. Competition between each pole will grow as the comparative advantage of one over another diminishes and, at times, unemployment and inflation may both become substantial in some countries. These pressures will highlight the need for multinational political arrangements on trade, arbitration of investment disputes, and the financial system to strengthen economic fairness and openness.

Significantly, most of the leaders of the most powerful economies agree that the means of preventing their nations from becoming homes for tens of millions of permanently unemployed is through strengthening global arrangements for fair and open world trade and investment. The populations of America, Japan, and Western

Europe dare not become the victims of unfair trade practices pursued by emerging economies. The key is to change the practices in the Third World, not resort to unfair trade in the First World.

Only by encouraging global investment on fair, competitive terms can the developing countries secure their economic potential. If they do not, they will be unable to offer decent prospects for their growing populations. In turn, the failure of the emerging economies to grow rapidly may be seen vividly in the form of millions of people seeking to escape from these countries and migrating north to the traditionally rich industrial countries.

The rapid advances of the Third World do not mean the demise of the First World. We do not deny that some American, European, and Japanese jobs will go to nations where wage rates are lower and productivity levels are impressive. Indeed, this has been happening for more than two decades. As this happens, the nature of the most developed economies changes. They become more services-driven and less manufacturing-based. There is nothing wrong with this in an era where the demands for all manner of services are rising rapidly from people who are wealthier and living longer.

The prospects for the advanced industrial countries to compete effectively and prosper in the coming Industrial Revolution are based in part on the vigor with which central banks in the industrial countries are fighting inflation and in part on policies, technologies, and management approaches that are giving major firms great scope to innovate.

It is the convergence of growth in the First World and the Third World—and the growing recognition of the dynamics of a multipolar, growth-oriented world—that sets the base for exceptional momentum in the international economy as the new century dawns.

Part II

Risks, Values, and Opportunities

8

Politics and
Corporate Reputation

e have presented our argument for the indisputability of the boom; there should no longer be any doubts about the enormous growth that is taking place in the emerging economies, a growth that is creating new potential for world leadership and economic achievement. You also know that there are incredible possibilities for success in the world's new poles for those who capitalize on this growth. Before we begin discussing the specific strategies for attaining success and creating wealth in the 21st century, we need to address one more set of "global" topics: those that shape the broad environment in which the boom will unfold and the second Industrial Revolution will emerge. These topics are: politics and corporate reputation, corruption and partnership, and militarism and capitalism. We start with politics and reputation.

One of the natural subplots of the second Industrial Revolution is the new political era it will unleash. It will have international and national features. The rapidly emerging nations will strive to secure a stronger place for themselves in international politics, while within their own countries their citizens will aspire to ever-greater involvement in governance.

A new political era is unfolding. For instance, more governments than ever will be openly and freely elected by the majority of the peoples. Already, free elections are taking place in nations with long traditions of dictatorships—from Malawi to Chile and from Russia to Albania. In Africa alone, more than 20 countries have introduced multi-party politics in the last five years. Many of these new democracies are fragile, the important institutions of democracy still young and uncertain: the judiciary is not entirely independent, the press is cautious and fearful of censorship, and the creation of new political parties is difficult.

In addition, in many countries, the dynamism of the new economic era will bring to power new leaders, more socially sensitive and more willing to challenge old, established elites to open their societies and find ways to arrest domestic poverty. Conversely, political uncertainties of all types will also abound, as the boom highlights growing divides between rich and poor and creates opportunities for radical populist groups to exploit the poor for political gains.

The new Industrial Revolution also means that more people will have disposable income and the ability to purchase cars, microwave ovens, fancy jewelry, and other items once considered luxuries. Indeed, within a generation, the world's largest automobile plants will probably be in China, the largest single national market for gold could be India, and some of the biggest assembly plants for home appliances could be in Pakistan and Brazil. As these countries prosper and as their economies become more integrated with those of other nations, their governments will inevitably demand from the Western industrial nations a greater say in global political affairs.

> "Within a generation, the world's largest automobile plants will probably be in China."

These demands will increasingly shape international relations in the first quarter of the 21st century. Growing economic prosperity will make the emerging nations more confident in dealing with the United States, Japan, and the European Union. A new assertiveness is already evident. For example, Japanese journalist Yoichi Funabashi has observed:

> Asia will no longer put up with being treated simply as a card: It will now demand respect as a player. Its success stories are likely to inspire and provide the voice for original, distinctly Asian ideas on a host of issues: human rights; the debate over democracy versus economic development; the relationship of corporate enterprises to the state, individuals to society, and society to the state; and security in the new world order and in the region.[1]

FREE MARKET HUMANISM

The peoples of the world's fastest developing countries will also want a greater voice in national politics. How they find this voice is difficult to predict. In many Third World countries and in Eastern and Central Europe today, it appears that people are searching for approaches that are neither socialist or staunchly capitalist. They are searching for models of democracy that might be different from those that we enjoy in the United States and in Western Europe.

However, it is becoming ever more evident that the increasingly affluent peoples of the emerging nations are seeking a greater say in how they are governed. They will want their booming economies to deliver the kinds of social dividends—better education, health care, social services—that governments are delivering in, for example, South Korea, Singapore, Taiwan, and Hong Kong. Increasingly, people in the Third World are appreciating that, to secure such benefits, they must create approaches that provide business with growth opportunities: respect and reward for individual enterprise; fair, equitable, and clear regulation (including ample self-regulation) of business; export promotion and rising levels of trade with the West; policies that secure open and well functioning financial markets (including securities markets); and measures that encourage foreign direct investment.

This combination of public demands for social dividends and public respect for open market economic systems might be called free market humanism. It is a model that could emerge widely and combine the best of socialism and capitalism. The desire to find approaches that mix the benefits of free enterprise with a profound concern for the welfare of the great mass of people is repeatedly given expression in speeches by such leaders as President Havel in the Czech Republic and President Mandela in South Africa.[2] The rhetoric of free market humanism has been put into practice in the newly industrializing countries of Asia, and it is spreading to other parts of the globe.

President Zedillo in Mexico is under public pressure to provide just this kind of new politics, and, indeed, an increasing number of Latin America's leaders are striving to find their own formulas to respond to public demands. President Frei in Chile has forged ahead with a model that places social justice and free enterprise side by side. Bolivia, a small and very poor country, has adopted a unique form of privatization that it calls "capitalization," which is nothing less than the quest to find a human framework for capitalism. The country's oil and gas, telephones, electricity, railways, refineries, and airline are being transferred from public to private ownership. Shares in each of these industries will be given to the country's 3.2 million people over the age of 21, while foreign direct investors have been invited to purchase up to 50 percent of the equity in these enterprises and, in turn, obtain full management control. The shares granted to the public will be the financial base for a strong pension system. The scheme is a start towards bringing one of the poorest countries in the Western Hemisphere onto the road of industrialization and private enterprise in a way that secures real benefits for all of its citizens. It might just work.[3]

New Technology and Politics

Ways of doing business by multinational corporations and investment decisions by individuals across the globe will be influenced by the international and domestic political developments that the boom will unleash. Making the whole scenario still more complicated and fascinating is the fact that new technologies will also have a profound impact on the new political climate.

As the economies of the world are being linked by new technologies, these new systems of communication and information are having a profound, transnational, political impact. A foretaste of the power of new technologies on politics was seen in the 1980s in Eastern Europe, when the communist leaders were unable to stop Western video and audio news and information from reaching their citizens. The impact on demands for change was enormous. Today, nonofficial political organizations across the Third World are linked by e-mail and Internet to similar entities in the West, and the result is a dramatic rise in the power of pressure groups on politics in emerging economies.

An example of the effect technology is having on politics is provided by the work being done by environmental groups. In most developing countries, the levels of environmental regulation are low relative to those that exist in North America and Western Europe. Even where significant regulations do exist, the resources to enforce them are frequently lacking. This situation is as much the product of inadequate general sensitivity to ecological issues as it is of concern that environmental regulation adds significant costs to business and to an economy as a whole, which poor countries cannot afford. In increasing numbers of developing countries today, however, not-for-profit, nongovernmental organizations are actively pressuring public authorities to preserve the environment.

From the Amazon in Brazil, where major road construction through Rondonia was halted by environmental activists, to the Namada Dam project in India, which lost international financial support because of environmental groups, these nongovernmental entities are on the march. They are demanding that politicians and civil servants explain their actions and policies to the public, that they consult with interest groups and local community groups, and that they adhere to new, higher levels of public accountability that, until now, have been unique to North America and Western Europe.

As the global information networks buzz, they influence the political agendas in the Third World and, in turn, directly impact the ways in which multinational corporations must behave. The impact is increasing. Today, if a U.S. company acts in ways viewed as counter to the public interest on the environmental front in Latin America, nongovernmental organizations in the region will alert their North American network counterparts, who, in turn, may alert activist shareholders. As a result, the company will find itself facing publicity problems at home because of actions it has taken thousands of miles away.

To an increasing degree, this type of global networking by interest groups is forcing corporations to accept the reality that they can no longer apply one set of environmental (or employment, or public policy) standards in one country and a much different and lower set of standards in another. These trends will become more pronounced in coming years.

Partnership and Corporate Attitudes

Relationships between multinational corporations, governments, and the citizens in emerging nations are going to be all the more complicated because of the scale of the political changes that are taking place. The forms that these relationships take will be crucial to all parties. The new political era will demand, for example, that corporations avoid actions that could lead to them being perceived as patronizing, neo-colonialist, or arrogant. Their success will come through new forms of partnership with these governments.

In striving to become more competitive, increasing numbers of firms will learn that staying national and dealing only in one cultural arena curtails their options on an ongoing basis. However, to maximize their options—that is, to go global—decision-makers must personally invest in learning the appropriate ways to behave in target countries and about the politics of the emerging economies. They must learn to listen to potential partners and to host country officials. Most importantly, they must understand what new forms of partnership are all about. The costs of failing on this front can be high.

Before an investment of cash is made in a new market, an investment of time and attitude is imperative. Attitude—moving into new markets with integrity and transparent motivation—is respect. Investing to secure respect from new business partners sounds obvious, yet too often it is done late and on too meager a level, and the results are less beneficial than wiser approaches would have yielded.

> **"There are still too many executives who are arrogant and dictatorial in dealing with potential partners"**

Today, most governments will give foreign business people more access and more time than ever before. In return, they expect foreign investors to show respect. The days when leaders of emerging nations would act as supplicants to investors from Japan, North America, and Western Europe, are gone. The imperial executive from the multinational corporation finds doors closed to him in countries whose booming economies are generating self-confidence. Unfortunately, however, there are still too many executives who appear too arrogant and dictatorial when they meet with potential business associates in developing countries. The costs of such behavior can be high, in terms of the opportunities lost and in terms of the lack of respect secured among local decision makers, both of which can impact the course of negotiations and the eventual deals that are completed.

A major Canadian mining company, for example, lost a gold concession in Africa, in part because its executives believed they could dictate the terms of the contract to the host government. Although they already had a good agreement, they went back to renegotiate and seek still better terms for themselves. Their arrogance ended in their demise. To the surprise of the Canadians, the Africans did not bend over backwards and change their systems to secure the Canadian investment cash; instead, they found alternative, less arrogant, foreign investors.

In some developing countries, multinational corporations have been seen as the new colonial powers, and their local representatives as the new commissioners from the colonial capitals. This view prevails in many political, media, and academic circles in emerging economies and in Central and Eastern Europe. The behavior of multinational firms in developing countries is critical in determining whether host governments view them as partners or as suspect beasts. If the latter, then regulations will emerge to limit the business scope of multinationals, and the real costs of this will fall most heavily on the citizenry of these protectionist countries. Economic deregulation that fosters the import of foreign technology, capital, and competition can provide substantial economic benefits. To curtail regulatory reform because foreign firms are seen as suspect would be tragic.

The Image of Multinationals

The idea that multinational corporations are creatures of the universe bound to no single, sovereign authority is a myth. In truth, multinational corporations are almost always closely identified with the countries in which their headquarters are located. Thus, companies like Coca-Cola and IBM are readily identified as U.S. companies, even though their non-U.S. operations are larger than their U.S. activities. There are exceptions, of course, as multinationals with headquarters in small countries may sometimes be less identified with their country of home origin than those that hail from large countries. Thus, ABB or Nestlé, both with headquarters in Switzerland, are seen more as European firms in general, rather than being closely identified with their Swiss base. By and large, however, governmental regulators, public interest groups of all kinds, investors, and business competitors associate Sony, Toshiba, and Hitachi with Japan, just as they associate Exxon with the U.S. and Daimler-Benz with Germany.

In most emerging economies, therefore, multinationals are seen by authorities, suppliers, labor groups, and other interest groups as foreign. This identification places a particular burden on the multinational. It demands of its managers that they behave as "guests" in countries in which the firm operates. They must behave well, because as foreigners they will be more heavily scrutinized than local enterprises. Their domestic competitors will seek to find fault with the guests and perhaps exploit this within a domestic political context. Moreover, their behavior may influence legislation that directly concerns their market access and opportunity.

Reputation Management

To maximize opportunities and be seen as guests, the multinational corporation must, above all, create an image for itself in its new markets as a genuine partner. It must impress upon host governments, customers, suppliers, and the public at large that it seeks a fair, open, long-term set of relationships.

Coca-Cola, for example, has repeatedly demonstrated around the world that it recognizes that, to establish this image, it must invest heavily and consistently in reputation management. It trains its staff to learn about the traditions, the politics, and the values of the people in all of the countries in which it operates. It gives key responsibilities to nationals of these countries and ensures that its image is the opposite of a ruthless, multinational, colonialist corporation.

Coca-Cola goes even further, in fact. It plays a full role in most of the countries in which it works, supporting education, the arts, and social services in a long-term and genuine way. Coca-Cola understands that the key to its success is its determination to show all of its business partners, no matter what their traditions and nationalities, that this company values integrity and understands the language of partnership and respect. This attitude garners admiration from its host countries.

Levi Strauss & Co., with 1993 global revenues of around $ 5.9 billion, produces in 76 plants in 24 countries and sells to more than 60 countries. It understands the importance of ensuring that hosts in foreign countries understand its values from the outset of forging a new relationship. In its public corporate statements, Levi Strauss has issued the following Guidelines for Country Selection:

> The following country selection criteria address issues which we believe are beyond the ability of the individual business partner to control.
>
> 1. Brand image. We will not initiate or renew contractual relationships in countries where sourcing would have an adverse effect on our global brand image.
> 2. Health and safety. We will not initiate or renew contractual relationships in locations where there is evidence that Company employees or representatives would be exposed to unreasonable risk.
> 3. Human rights. We will not initiate or renew contractual relationships in countries where there are pervasive violations of basic human rights.
> 4. Legal requirements. We will not initiate or renew contractual relationships in countries where the legal environment creates unreasonable risk to our trademarks or to other important commercial interests or seriously impedes our ability to implement these guidelines.
> 5. Political and social stability. We will not initiate or renew contractual relationships in countries where political or social turmoil unreasonably threatens our commercial interests.[4]

Clarity like that which Levi Strauss illustrates here is a key to partnership, building trust, and winning respect.

On entering a country for the first time to do business, a corporation must ensure that all its contacts understand that it will be keen to invest for the long-term in ways that are totally open and above board. If the potential foreign investor does not state from the outset its general beliefs and approaches, it may find its hosts swiftly testing it to determine if extortion opportunities exist. In the very first round of meetings with government officials and local businessmen, one may encounter a suggestion about the fast way to achieve action, as distinct from the bureaucratic and slow way. In other words, if the multinational pays the bribes, it will get results; if not, nothing will happen. Avoid these situations by making your ethical intent known. No deal is so valuable that a corporation should risk its reputation on it. We will discuss corruption in detail in the next chapter.

Although there are still few companies around the globe that have heard this message, General Mills is an exception. In its corporate public statement on responsibility, it declares:

> Obeying the law is a minimum. Ethical business conduct should normally exist at a level well above the minimum required by law and company policy. One of the most valuable assets is our reputation for integrity. If that is tarnished, customers, investors, and desirable employees will seek affiliation with other, more attractive companies. We intend to hold to a single standard of integrity everywhere. We will keep our word. We will not promise more than we can reasonably hope to deliver, nor will we make commitments we do not intend to keep.[5]

The new investor in a foreign country must make clear its willingness to make a substantial, long-term commitment to the country, which will translate into foreign exchange earnings and the creation of jobs. But this commitment must be contingent upon the ability to operate in the country in an open and transparent manner. Making this statement early in discussions with officials can have a positive impact. Foreign executives are often too slow to state this and, by default, local individuals assume that the foreign executive is open to corrupt dealings.

Ciba-Geigy of Switzerland, one of the largest pharmaceutical companies in the world, has developed public statements that seek to precisely articulate its stance which it shares with officials in developing countries as soon as it arrives. With regard to its activities in these countries, the Ciba-Geigy statement says:

> Ciba acts in partnership with developing countries to advance their economic potential in the interest of both parties. It fully observes the rights and duties arising out of such a partnership. In making business decisions about the developing world—for example, about

products, services, technologies, and investments—Ciba takes into account their impact on the development of the host country in addition to economic criteria. Ciba is prepared to take a long-term view of profit in developing countries.[6]

The basic lesson to be drawn from the example of the leading multinational corporations is this: shape public affairs and image-enhancing approaches to local customs and cultures. Corporations need to learn the ways and mores of the new society they have entered. They cannot afford to overlook detailed information on local customs, because even the smallest matters can have an impact. Earning the goodwill of host governments and host country business organizations is crucially important for the establishment of a multinational enterprise and its future success in particular countries. The issue is not one of charity or of doing good for the sake of doing good; rather, it is an issue of investing wisely and well to build goodwill.

There are many companies that have been asked in subtle ways to leave a country because their expatriate employees tried to

> "Multinational corporations must learn the ways and mores of new societies and shape public affairs to local customs and cultures."

smuggle goods through airport customs, got into fights with local nationals, committed minor, local crimes, or were drunk in public places. These companies found that government agencies were no longer doing business with them, and they found it difficult to get work permits renewed and business license applications dealt with in a timely fashion. They encountered all manner of minor irritations that made doing business impossible, thus forcing them to leave the country.

Few corporations have better understood all of these factors and their increasing importance than Coca-Cola. It does not pay bribes, it does not act like a colonial power in the Third World, its top executives do not act arrogantly when visiting developing countries, and it undertakes a vast number of actions to demonstrate to its foreign hosts that it is a committed, long-term investor. In short, Coca-Cola acts as a partner.[7]

Coca-Cola's View of Partnership

The following paragraphs are taken directly from the September 1993 edition of Coca-Cola's *Journey* magazine:

A Pattern of Partnership

Across China, the Coca-Cola system is expanding to serve customers and consumers through a network of partnerships with key bottlers and government agencies. Most bottlers are run as joint ventures between system veterans—the company, other bottlers, or both—and various governmental based operators. Others are state-owned, in a nation long praised for an infrastructure and distribution system that feeds 1.2 billion people every day.

In either case, Coca-Cola is an important part of China's economic progress, which has grabbed the attention of the financial world. The Chinese economy, growing at 9 percent annually, is now ranked third-largest in the world.

"The open door policy of China is exactly to try and bring in expertise from abroad. That is one of the premises on which we base this cooperation with The Coca-Cola Company," said Madame Pan Beilei, vice-minister of the Chinese General Council of Light industry, one of the Company's joint-venture partners.

"The cooperation we have in mind is very sincere, and the result will be mutually beneficial," she said during a recent visit to Company headquarters. "Your company has a high level of expertise and high product quality. Through our cooperation, we hope you will promote development of the beverage industry in China."

Using beverage concentrate produced at the Company's Shanghai facility, Coca-Cola, Sprint, and Fanta are produced at plants from Beijing to Haikou and are sold by a wide variety of customers—from state stores to private entrepreneurs, from large grocers to mom-and-pop stores and coffee shops. Jinmeile, the Chinese brand produced in the Company's Tianjin joint venture, also helps develop the local beverage industry in China.

Following Words with Actions

Declarations of fundamental corporate ethics start to bite when the companies that issue them also demonstrate that they act upon them. It is all too easy for companies to talk about acting ethically and, to be sure, many individuals and firms will have different perspectives on just what "acting ethically" means. Levi Strauss has stated its view through its actions and, while its approaches may have caused unpopularity in some quarters, they have boosted respect for the firm in others. For example, Levi Strauss has stated that it will not work in countries where there are pervasive violations of human rights. Accordingly, it determined in 1992 not to do business in Myanmar, and, one year later, it withdrew from China for similar reasons.

Levi Strauss's mission statement highlights a philosophy that is very much in accord with the political dynamics and value systems evident in increasing numbers of emerging countries. It is a statement that makes this corporation welcome in many foreign countries:

> The mission of Levi Strauss & Co. is to sustain responsible commercial success as a global marketing company of branded casual apparel. We must balance goals of superior profitability and return on investment, leadership market positions, and superior products and service. We will conduct our business ethically and demonstrate leadership in satisfying our responsibilities to our communities and to society. Our work environment will be safe and productive and characterized by fair treatment, teamwork, open communications, personal accountability, and opportunities for growth and development.[8]

Levi Strauss places its corporate integrity and its determination to earn respect above all other criteria. In so doing, it sets a standard, and it is likely to win wider respect in a world where economic change is swift and is forcing political change that will demand new, high standards of behavior and partnership from multinational corporations. Levi Strauss is not alone, but there are not enough companies that follow a similar path or adequately understand the motivations behind the issue of responsibility statements. More countries need to recognize that the way forward for multinational corporations in the 21st century is through open and honest partnerships.

9

Corruption Risks and Business Partnerships

Corruption, the abuse of public power for private gain, exists on a massive scale in much of global commerce. It is a factor in many of the largest infrastructure projects in the Third World. It is a factor in many arms deals between nations. It is also a factor in obtaining important government contracts in numerous industrial countries, as recent major scandals have shown in Italy, Spain, Belgium, and France. The opportunities for corruption may increase as the second Industrial Revolution evolves and global investment and trade volumes mount. Unless checked, corruption could pose a threat to the boom scenario in many countries, undermining and distorting competitive and open economies.

Corruption is so widespread because business people and politicians believe they can get away with it. Many corporations bribe because they believe their competitors are offering bribes, so they rationalize that they have no choice but to use the tools of corruption when seeking contracts. British industrialist Lord Young[1] told the BBC that British companies have to bribe in some areas of the world where such payments are accepted as part of the traditional culture. Many European companies assert that they must pay bribes to win foreign contracts. Moreover, they claim tax deductions

> "Corruption exists on a massive scale and could pose a threat to the boom scenario."

for these illicit payments, and they lobby their politicians to ensure these tax benefits remain in place. In fact, the United States is the only country that currently has a law on the books making it a criminal offense for a firm to pay bribes abroad to win contracts.

While bribery may be a way of life for many multinational corporations and the scale of bribery may be mounting, the rising material and educational levels of the citizens of most developing countries are generating increased calls for publicly accountable politicians and civil servants. More independent newspapers are being created, more vocal, nongovernmental organizations are being established, and pressures are mounting for more independent judicial systems. The era of economic liberalization—which is seeing deregulation in multinational trade, finance, and investment, and greater labor movement across national borders—is prompting an era of enhanced political liberalization.

In this chapter, we provide illustrations of current corruption issues, and we highlight the important linkages between growing corruption and successful economic growth and between corruption and building democratic societies where human rights are respected. We also highlight the positive efforts now being made to counter the cancer of corruption. As we have already stressed, we believe few issues will be more important to growth in the emerging economies and in Central and in Eastern Europe than the curbing of corruption. Though many multinational corporations have used bribes to win foreign business in the past, the risks of this behavior are growing in increasing numbers of countries, and the chances of success based on corruption are decreasing. Successful business in the 21st century will be accomplished through honest partnerships, not under-the-table kickbacks.

The Situation in Eastern and Central Europe

If there are any doubts about the growth of corruption, then a short look at the events in Eastern and Central Europe will dispel them. The hesitation on the part of many business people about prospects for this region derives largely from the current conditions of corruption. In September 1993, the European Bank for Reconstruction and Development (EBRD)[2] published its annual economic review of the region, and it decided to cast diplomatic language aside. It saw the region facing collapse, because the essential ethical culture upon which business must be based in order to succeed in the long-term was absent.

The EBRD concluded that the government bureaucracy and prevailing attitudes and practices represented enormous hurdles for the entrepreneur to surmount. The activity of "rent seeking" is costing enterprises time and money and, thus, is costing society valuable resources. The study went on to stress that:

> If, in addition, the entrepreneur expects to have to give a 'cut' of the enterprise to a variety of claimants—outside fees to governments, bribes to public servants, payments to protection racketeers, and so forth—and to allocate time to reach a deal with each of them, the total transaction costs may be even larger, and the disincentive to proceed with the project may well be far greater.

The EBRD declared that:

> These obstacles to the autonomy of private enterprises have long been identified as a major deterrent to inward foreign investment in the region ... the phenomenon of bribe-seeking and protection rackets are side-effects of the introduction of capitalism into a situation of economic under-development.

There are businessmen who return from the former Soviet Union, for example, with tales of the two ways of doing business: the official and tedious way, which often seems like a journey without end and the crooked route. Peter Hack, Member of Parliament in Hungary, puts it bluntly, "Eastern European countries are facing the biggest changes in their history. There is virtually no stable element; change must be made in every area. Corruption is everywhere."

A Spreading Virus

Corruption is widespread in many parts of the Third World. As is evident in Nigeria and Zaire, where authoritarian governments, who use terror to secure their power, have no qualms about taking bribes. New opportunities for corruption are surfacing in countries where socialism is breaking down and dynamic capitalism is raging. China is an example of this. In the last three to four years, the spread of corruption in China has been so substantial that it has strengthened fears that a period of severe political and economic strain will occur in the immediate future. Corruption is also coming to the fore in countries where whole new middle classes are being formed, as economic policies of deregulation are rapidly being introduced and new rules of the game have yet to be firmly established. Here, India is a case in point. Corruption has long been widespread among the lower levels of the civil service in India, but the new economic boom is generating all manner of new business opportunities that, to some extent, are proving too tempting for many senior civil servants and politicians.

The size of the payments made to win contracts varies enormously. For example, in July 1994, two executives of a European bank were forced to resign when it was revealed that they had been involved in bribery in Malaysia. Apparently, the bank, upon investigating the disappearance of $10,000 worth of gold coins, determined that the bullion division of one of its subsidiaries had apparently given these to a Malaysian minister as a "trade sample"!

George Moody-Stewart, a retired British businessman with decades of experience in Africa and Asia, states that an under-the-table payment of 5% to a head of government in the Third World on a large contract used to be typical, but, recently, figures like 10% and 15% are often heard. He adds that:

> Recent years have seen a huge increase in corruption and fraud in the developing world. We are not talking about theft, or the actions of petty officials in many countries who look for bribes for doing or not doing their jobs. What concerns me is the corruption of officials, ministers, and heads of state, whose decisions can greatly influence the development of the Third World. I call this Grand Corruption.[3]

Taking a Stand Against Corruption

There may well be many developing countries that move slowly in creating more transparent societies where corruption is a thing of the past. Indeed, many currently powerful politicians are resisting pressures to be more open and accountable, and they may resort to locking up their perceived critics, or even to violence. Despite this, greater transparency and open, full partnerships in politics and business is inevitable.

Concern over corruption is leading to a host of new initiatives. At the national level, an array of new political parties and non-governmental organizations is growing up in Asia, Africa, and Latin America (and no doubt in Eastern and Central Europe before too long) whose top priority is ensuring that corruption is confronted by the judicial and political systems. In Western Europe, following scandals in numerous countries, greater efforts than ever before are being made to change laws that enable multinational companies to receive tax deductions for their foreign bribes. These efforts may be the first stage in a series of actions designed to make the payment of foreign bribes a crime. In the U.S., the Foreign Corrupt Practices Act (FCPA), passed in 1977, makes it a criminal offense for U.S. firms to pay bribes abroad. Unfortunately, many U.S. businesses either circumvent this law or complain bitterly that it places them at a disadvantage against their Japanese and West European competitors. For example, in late 1994, Lockheed Corporation settled a FCPA case with the Department of Justice with a fine of over $24 million.

On the other hand, many U.S. companies are taking the high road in being at the forefront of international efforts to see FCPA-type legislation accepted in all countries. General Electric, AIG, Enron, Boeing, and Westinghouse are among the founding U.S. members of Transparency International, a global coalition to curb corruption in international business transactions, which we discuss below.

Moreover, U.S. Secretary of State Warren Christopher has launched efforts to promote action through the OECD. The Secretary told businessmen in late October 1993 that:

> Our companies are losing hundreds of millions of dollars in contracts every year because their non-American competitors are able to bribe foreign officials, while American companies are bound by the Foreign Corrupt Practices Act ... what we want to press for is what the OECD is doing, and that is considering and pushing an initiative to recommend to its member nations that they have measures to prevent their companies from making illicit payments.

TRANSPARENCY INTERNATIONAL

As we have mentioned, measures to curb corruption are being taken at the international level. Transparency International (TI)[4] was established in May 1993 by a group of individuals, many of whom had worked for international aid organizations and in business in the Third World, who shared the conviction that pragmatic actions could be taken in many countries to counter the rising tide of corruption in international business transactions. The enthusiasm generated, in particular, by TI's Chairman, Peter Eigen, who had spent more than 25 years working for the World Bank, won support from national aid agencies in the U.S., Canada, Scandinavia, France, Germany, the Netherlands, and the U.K., from several major corporations, some foundations (notably the Ford Foundation), and from such prominent individuals as former U.S. Secretary of Defense Robert McNamara and Costa Rican Nobel prize winner Oscar Arias. TI is a nonprofit, nongovernmental organization whose mission is to:

- curb corruption through international coalitions assisting governments to establish and implement effective laws, policies, and anti-corruption programs;
- strengthen public support and understanding for anti-corruption programs that enhance public transparency and accountability in international business transactions;
- encourage all parties in international business transactions to operate at the highest levels of integrity, guided by the mandates in TI's Standards of Conduct.

To achieve these goals, TI's basic operational strategy is to:

- establish coalitions of like-minded organizations and individuals to work with governments that invite TI to assist in designing and implementing national anti-corruption programs;
- establish close ties to the media, participate in public fora, and use publicity campaigns to broaden public awareness of the damage caused by corruption, the need to counter it, and the means to reduce it;
- build national chapters of TI that foster anti-corruption actions in their own country and secure support for TI's international operations.

Transparency International's establishment reflects a judgement by many experts that, if ever there was a time to strive and make a difference on this front, it is now. At TI's launch conference in

Berlin in May 1993, Robert McNamara asserted there is more chance now of effectively attacking major corruption than at any time in his almost 50 years of professional life. He said, "The subject of corruption could not have been discussed (in official international fora) 20, 15, or even five years ago."

In part, this is due to the political development of the emerging countries themselves, but it is also a reaction to the greed of the 1980s, which saw corruption become so massive and widespread that it became a patently visible threat to economic growth and political development. The ending of the Cold War also contributed, because it forced Western aid agencies to focus more on the economic impact of aid and, therefore, on corruption's impact, than on the earlier priority of winning political friends in the East-West confrontation.

National Actions Against Corruption

Public protests against corruption, often stimulated by media investigations and by courageous public prosecutors, have taken a rising toll. For example, in the leading industrial countries, politicians and businessmen have gone to jail in Italy, they have been disgraced in Japan, and they have been forced out of office in France.

In developing countries, the public debate over corruption has never been so open and widespread as it is today. Increasing numbers of politicians are concluding that it makes good political, economic, and social sense for them to take a stand against corruption. The new parties that formed in Kenya to oppose President Moi saw their fundamental public appeal as being concerned with honesty in government. In Malawi, the first open, multi-party elections saw the ouster of President Banda—a vote against the man who ruled the nation since independence—an action that could only be interpreted as a plea by the mass of the population for greater public accountability on the part of politicians.

The impeachment of President Collor in Brazil did not end the issue of corruption in the political domain of that country; rather, it strengthened politicians who believe this is an issue of strong public appeal and one which, if promoted effectively, can lead to major changes in the nation's political landscape.

In Namibia, the need to take firm action to counter corruption and ensure against its increase was seen as a priority by the new, independent government. Arrangements have been put in place, both openly and through a judiciary seen to be independent and fair, to turn rhetoric on this front into action. Most notably, a Presidential Commission of Inquiry on Corruption has been established. Namibian Attorney General Hartmut Ruppel explains:

> "It makes good political, economical, and social sense to take a stand against corruption."

To fight corruption you have to change the environment. That requires a legal framework of tough laws and mechanisms to force open normally inaccessible transactions. We must strive to strike a fair balance between necessary measures and legitimate claims of confidentiality.

In Uganda, as well as in numerous other African countries, courageous political leaders are taking the lead in seeking to introduce reforms and new institutional arrangements that counter corruption. For example, the position and authority of the Inspector General in the Government of Uganda is being strengthened to provide the independence of action necessary to investigate all parts of the public sector. The efforts in Uganda are part of a sweeping program of constitutional reform and civil service overhaul involving the reduction of the public sector by two-thirds. There is an acute sensitivity on the part of the leadership that, while many actions can be taken to curb large-scale corruption and theft by people in top political positions, the reduction of invidious, small-scale corruption can be harder. In Uganda, as in so many other countries, civil servants are not paid a living wage, so the incentive to be dishonest is high. Part of the current Ugandan approach is to ensure that, within three years, all civil servants are on income levels above the minimum survival level. Singapore, for example, has one of the highest civil service pay scales in the world, and it also has one of the lowest levels of corruption.

In the Philippines, where former President Marcos's thefts still cast a long shadow on national politics, today's leadership has made the fight against corruption the central plank of its popular appeals. It may take many years to really secure change in the Philippines, but never before has the effort been as serious in that country as it is today.

Meanwhile, as corruption has grown and spread, central banks have started to coordinate actions to curb international money laundering. The fraud perpetrated by the Bank for Credit and Commerce International (BCCI) has strengthened the resolve of banking authorities to act. International security expert Michael Hershman, Chairman of the Fairfax Group, claims that the BCCI scandal:

> Proved to the banking community that it can no longer not ask questions. The Swiss and other countries' financial institutions are opening up. With new techniques and resources devoted to fighting corruption, it is going to be easier to undertake investigations. It is getting more difficult to hide the assets."[5]

Human Rights and Democracy

The mounting efforts to curb corruption reflect a growing understanding across the globe of the true political and social costs of bribery and kickbacks. Corruption is a humanitarian issue. Because of its prevalence, vast sums of money are

> "Corruption is a humanitarian issue. Corruption is the enemy of democracy."

misallocated by public officials in dozens of countries. Funds originally earmarked for new schools, hospitals, and institutions to serve the needy are often channeled into projects of negligible social value by officials receiving bribes from commercial contractors. This directly damages the economy. Lost are the opportunities to make people healthier and better educated and, thereby, more productive.

Corruption is the enemy of democracy. Corrupt leaders cling to power, opposing efforts to open government, curbing personal freedoms, and abusing basic human rights. Corruption crushes the potential benefits of free market forces. The honest business person goes broke, the rules of a healthy economic system become twisted, and companies addicted to paying bribes become rotten. In consequence, prospects for economic progress, so vital to social development, are ruined.

The most forthright abuses of political power for private gain take place in systems where vested interests are deeply entrenched and protected by special, government-supported cartel and monopoly arrangements. In such circumstances, the dealings made between private individuals and corrupt political leaders thrive, because public accountability and competition are both nonexistent. The establishment of more transparent systems, including the formation of a vibrant press, the establishment of competition, and the creation of a secure judicial system, is an essential requirement for building and sustaining democratic government.

The successful corporation in this new era will be the one that avoids bribery and seeks partnership, recognizing that open, honest, long-term commitments in the emerging economies are the soundest and surest roads to success. To operate profitably, corporations must change their approaches to competitiveness and their attitudes.

Corruption is a testing ground. Working hard to earn respect in foreign nations is a more cost-effective route to success than paying bribes. It is also right.

10

Militarism and Capitalism

The extent to which emerging economies spend their resources on defense will impact the pace of their economic advance. Their attitudes towards capitalism and providing free enterprise with room to develop will be just as important. For multinational corporations, and for all people seeking to understand the implications of the new Industrial Revolution, the issues of militarism and capitalism are central.

Military Spending

The continuing uncertainties in the political and economic climate in Central and Eastern Europe make it imprudent to rule out a revival of massive arms spending by some countries that could distort the global economy and stimulate some developing countries to devote major slices of national income to arms, thereby undermining their own growth.

The International Monetary Fund estimates[1] that world military spending fell at an annual rate of almost 20 percent from the late 1980s, and it posed the question of what would happen if this formidable rate of decline continued. It answered by noting that, initially, lower military spending reduces economic growth, but it then paves the way for reduced taxes, better fiscal balance, and new opportunities for the private sector to raise capital. The peace dividend created by reduced arms spending could run into hundreds of billions of dollars.

The gains for developing countries vary greatly depending on current levels of military spending, the degree to which these countries import arms, and the extent to which such spending is a major, public sector, financial drain. In almost all countries, arms spending cuts will reduce budget deficits and curb interest rate rises,

ARMS TRADE 1988–1992 EXPORTERS, IMPORTERS ($MILLIONS)

Top Exporters	Total 1988–1992	Top Importers	Total 1988–1992
USA	54,968	India	12,235
Former USSR	45,182	Japan	9,224
France	9,349	Saudi Arabia	8,690
Germany	8,190	Afghanistan	7,515
China	7,658	Greece	6,197
U.K.	7,623	Turkey	6,197
Czechoslovakia	3,163	Iraq	4,967
Netherlands	2,048		
Italy	1,613	Sweden	1,416
Brazil	1,028		
TOTAL	151,014	TOTAL	151,014

In addition, estimates of global military assistance indicate that in 1993 the Former Soviet Union spent no money on arms, compared with $13.5 billion in 1987. Other 1993 figures include: US $3.4 billion; Western Europe, $900 million; Arab States, $200 million; and China, $100 million.[6]

thereby yielding both direct and indirect formidable economic benefits, and increasing the availability of global investment funds for nonmilitary purposes. In recent times, the trends for global spending on arms have been declining, but the scale of outlays remains very high: Between 1987 and 1991, global military spending fell from $995 billion to $855 billion (in the industrial countries the drop was nearly 15 percent, from $850 billion to $725 billion, while for the developing countries the fall was barely 10 percent, from $145 billion to $130 billion).[2]

> "The peace dividend created by reduced arms spending could run into hundreds of billions of dollars."

Nonetheless, the increasing prosperity of emerging economies and the integration of the world economy combine to make the world of the 21st century a more dangerous place. Wolfgang H. Reinicke, of the Brookings Institution, notes:

The ever-increasing trade in goods and technologies that have both commercial and military uses seems to mock the goal of keeping dangerous products out of dangerous hands. Not only has there been a sharp increase in what is known as 'foreign availability' of weapons technology; increasingly, countries are able to produce their own proscribed weapons by piecemealing—manufacturing weapons after buying different parts from different countries.[3]

It would be folly to make predictions. At the moment, however, it appears that China, India, Pakistan, and numerous countries in Central and Eastern Europe, the Middle East, and Latin America (notably Brazil) have substantial arms industries. These arms industries may be expanded even further for national security reasons or to meet demands from foreign powers. The most advanced industrial countries have only marginal leverage today to influence the military spending of these emerging economies and, as these economies grow stronger, the leverage will decline further.

As we have already noted, within a couple of decades China may be the world's most powerful economy. This position may encourage its leaders to be more forceful in the arena of international political relations. China's historic interests in Asia have not been forgotten by Asia's residents, and, indeed, there is already concern in sophisticated political circles about the potential military threat that China could pose. Quoted in *Foreign Affairs* magazine in

> **"The world in the 21st century will be a more dangerous place."**

December 1993, for example, Singapore's Lee Kuan Yew said:

> The size of China's displacement of the world balance is such that the world must find a new balance in 30 to 40 years. It's not possible to pretend that this is just another big player. This is the biggest player in the history of man.[4]

If China and the other new powers emerging in the Third World want to maintain and expand foreign investor confidence, they will need to find ways to control their armed forces and the politicians who may have expansionist ambitions. Their challenge may be difficult at times, and monitoring developments will become extremely important. It can be argued that foreign policy leaders in Europe and the United States have paid insufficient attention to the military implications presented by new, huge, economic powers in parts of the developing world and the establishment of new forms of sharing global power.

Defense and Infrastructure Capital

In terms of securing their nonmilitary, public spending goals, emerging countries have much to lose by embarking on major arms spending programs. Arms spending can boost budget deficits and weaken foreign investor interest in countries. Arms spending can boost national debts by draining vital domestic savings needed for new roads, railways, and other infrastructure improvements, forcing governments to borrow more money.

The militarism issue is particularly difficult to grapple with in Central and Eastern Europe. Although military spending in parts of this region has declined sharply in recent years, it could rise again. The relationships between the newly independent states are fragile. Today, Ukraine, Russia, and Belarus appear to be moving closer to each other, with the recognition that, together, they can gain far more. However, political and economic conditions are so uncertain that this trend could be swiftly reversed. Moreover, the serious threat of civil war exists in some of these countries, as the Chechnya independence efforts highlighted in Spring 1995.

The Military's New Role

There is yet another dimension to the militarism issue: the role of the military in the future. In the United States the military is assuming a larger role as a police force, such as in the cases of Haiti, Somalia, or Rwanda. In the former Soviet Union, diplomats and businessmen tell stories of the increasing partnership between the military and organized crime. One diplomat suggested that, when the Russians had a military base on German soil, they used it as a depot for stolen German cars, which were later transported by Russian military aircraft to central Russia for delivery to the mafia. The Mercedes automobiles were taken from the streets of Berlin and Hamburg, driven to the Russian military base, loaded on large cargo planes, and handed to the Russian mafia a few hours later!

Concerns will be raised in some developing countries about the degree to which the military can be trusted in the transition from largely dictatorship forms of government to more open, democratic forms. In the dictatorships, the military always had a clear role, and, in many cases, it even provided the dictator. In democracies, however, the political power of the military tends to be curbed. The frustrations of the military have repeatedly been seen in countries that have tried from time to time to become more politically democratic, such as Nigeria and Pakistan.

In coming years, as many countries enjoy unprecedented prosperity, governments seek to reduce military budgets to build more balanced budgets, and public demands for more open political systems rise, will military leaders quietly accept their diminishing roles?

There are no general, meaningful answers to this question. The pressures of rapid economic growth on all elements of society should not be underestimated, and, in many developing countries, they will undoubtedly lead to instability. Given that the instability in some countries may, in turn, unleash new demands for U.S. intervention, we must conclude that the prospects for further substantial reductions in U.S. military spending, over and above what is already planned, are marginal.

Overall, most people in most countries are likely to support political trends that continue to foster rapid rises in general living standards and peaceful transitions to more open forms of government. However, we believe that business people, with their habit of avoiding politics and often underestimating its power, must be increasingly sensitive to military factors when determining their strategies. They need to know, and constantly monitor, the risks they are facing in each country.

The Capitalism Issue

Political risk insurance is increasingly available to protect firms from expropriation, but this is not sufficient to make foreign businessmen confident. Governments that pursue patterns of nationalization will undermine their economies. Governments that demonstrate

respect for private property and work to attract foreign direct investment will reap rewards. This fact is more widely understood by
governments in the world today than at any other time in history.

To understand how this situation has arisen, we must look
back to the early 1980s, when the international investment environment was changed by the pro-private sector foreign policies
launched with steel determination by President Ronald Reagan of
the United States and Prime Minister Margaret Thatcher of the United
Kingdom and solidly supported by Chancellor Helmut Kohl in Germany. These leaders loathed socialism, and they believed they
could bankrupt communism. Their approach, which involved spending vast sums on an arms race and using every opportunity to undermine internal order within the Warsaw Pact area, contributed to
the ending of the Cold War.

These leaders were no less ruthless in dealing with the Third
World. Reagan and Thatcher led a foreign aid revolution that reversed the 1970s trend of increasing real volumes of aid flows,
curbed the level of foreign aid to most developing nations that
would not support the West's foreign policies, and made it increasingly clear that aid was not a source of charity, but a limited
source of conditional finance available for tightly proscribed purposes. Aid recipients got the message: For development to succeed,
the developing nations had to fling their borders open to foreign
private investment, and progress made on that front would be re-
warded by Western aid flows.

Never before had aid agencies been so blunt with the recipients
of their funds. Now, economic policy conditionality was everything,
with the exception of a few countries that the West felt were
strategically important in the Cold War, such as Zaire, Sudan, and
Somalia, all of which received U.S. aid for purely political purposes, with the funds often going into the foreign bank accounts
of the national leaders.

Prime Minister Thatcher was not tolerant of compromises or of
lengthy papers that explained the nuances of economic development. She believed aid should be granted only to countries that
opened their doors to international trade and competition, set free
exchange rates, balanced their budget books, controlled the money
supply, privatized public sector enterprises, streamlined the civil ser-

vice, and created an environment that was thoroughly attractive to foreign investors. President Reagan agreed, and the leading global aid agencies changed their policies as a result. Aid agencies declared that the promotion of such polices was "structural adjustment." For Reagan and Thatcher, the policies were better labeled capitalism.

For three decades, until the launch of the Reagan–Thatcher revolution, the industrial nations pursued foreign aid policies that provided support to the governments of developing countries and financed the construction of huge state enterprises. Money was spent on public works, from highways and ports to airports and sports stadiums. Health, education, and housing schemes were financed across Asia, Africa, and Latin America.

To be sure, there are countries that have failed to bring population growth and economic capacity into line, that have failed to secure decent education and health services, and that now confront new threats, such as AIDS. Then, there are countries that have been unable to establish stable political systems and countries that have been mired in absolute poverty resulting from civil wars or the actions of brutal regimes. While newspapers and television report almost daily on such situations, the reality is that, in recent decades, the scale of social and economic progress in much of the developing world has been impressive.[5]

These advances have played a fundamental role in setting the stage for economic lift-off and industrialization across the developing world. On their own, however, they would not have been enough to fuel the second Industrial Revolution. Reagan and Thatcher believed that the developing countries also had to marry social progress with capitalism.

The old aid policies, which steered clear of central issues of economic policy, supported huge public sector projects, and sought to be strictly neutral in terms of capitalism, were blasted by the men to whom Thatcher and Reagan listened. These individuals were led by Lord Bauer in the U.K., scholars at The Heritage Foundation in the U.S., and the editorial writers at *The Wall Street Journal*. These advisors ignored the benefits that aid had created, and they argued that the old style of aid did more damage than good. Aid was seen as: promoting corruption and undermining democracy; creating aid-dependence and robbing people of the incentives to be

enterprising; and securing the positions of vested interests in emerging nations, thereby reducing the forces of competition in those
economies and leading to greater impoverishment, especially
given the high birth rates in many nations.

These views gained popularity in the 1980s, as people across
the industrialized nations questioned the effectiveness of aid. Stories of Third World corruption were rampant. Television in Europe
and North America showed massive starvation in nations which had
received vast amounts of taxpayer financed Western aid. The crisis
in Ethiopia in the mid-1980s promoted a remarkable level of charitable giving, and it simultaneously raised calls in one parliament
after another: "What happened to our aid money?"

Calls for aid reform strengthened in the course of the 1980s:

1. There had to be less aid.

2. Aid programs had to be much more oriented to building
    free enterprise in developing countries, rather than to
    supporting big government.

3. Aid programs had to be far more sensitive to
    environmental issues.

4. Particularly as the Cold War ended, aid had to be used
    more directly to promote "good governance," involving the
    introduction of multiparty democracy.

Pressures for policies like these came at a time when the coffers of many Third World countries were empty. Partly encouraged
by Western governments and banks, these countries had amassed
vast debts.

Now, their export markets were shattered by world recession,
largely induced by anti-inflation policies spearheaded by the U.S.
Federal Reserve Board, so these poor Third World countries could
not service their foreign debts. These countries, pressured directly
by the White House and the International Monetary Fund, came to
understand that they had no choice other than to seek to attract
foreign private investment funds as part of a fundamental restructuring of their economies. By the end of the 1980s, the only
developing countries in the world that had not embraced this
view were Cuba and North Korea. Even Vietnam had caught the

capitalism bug and was active in inviting the world's biggest private enterprises to invest in Hanoi and Saigon and their environs.

The world had changed. Although conversion to free market policies was often initiated with reluctance and in the face of much domestic opposition, by the end of the 1980s most of the governments of the developing countries were pursuing policies of economic liberalization because they believed in them and because they were starting to secure ever deeper general public support. It was no longer a case of adopting capitalism simply to please the White House and the IMF. From Chile to the Czech Republic, from Mexico to India, the encouragement of foreign direct investment was at the forefront of economic policy design.

Implementation of these policies increasingly led to job creation and assured that capitalist approaches became firmly entrenched. The 1980s was a breathtaking period of policy change across the Third World. It changed politics profoundly. Trade unions with leftist views were in retreat. Talk of nationalization and building-up state enterprises was no longer heard. Governments that a decade earlier would not have dreamt or dared to advocate the sale to foreign private enterprises of the state telephone or power or airline company, were now doing precisely this and winning popular support as a result. From Argentina to Zambia, privatization became the fashion.

It is difficult against this background to envisage a fundamental

> "The 1980s was a breathtaking period of policy change across the Third World."

reversal. The modernization of the state, creating whole new opportunities for social and economic progress for individual citizens, is now firmly set on capitalist lines throughout the Third World. International business executives seeking new investment opportunities in these Third World countries need not fear expropriation (it is still far too early to make a similar statement with regard to most of Central and Eastern Europe, except Slovenia, the Czech Republic, and Hungary), and they can look forward to conditions of ever greater freedom of enterprise, trade, exchange rate convertibility, and investment.

However, the pace of economic development is so rapid that there will inevitably be times of political reverses, particularly when interest groups feel most challenged by the new pressures that economic dynamism unleashes. In coming years, the pace of the economic growth in many countries will directly undermine the dominance in many societies of small, exceptionally wealthy groups of individuals. How these individuals will react to the challenges remains to be seen. In some cases, they may resort to nondemocratic means to maintain their power, while in other cases they may simply be blown aside by the exceptional forces of rapidly rising middle-classes demanding a share of political power.

In periods of exceptional economic growth the benefits are not spread evenly to all peoples. There will be those who, seeing themselves bypassed, may be particularly attracted to politicians offering radical programs. The new economic era will be a period when leadership skills of many governments may be tested.

If, in this period ahead, governments can learn from the Asian experience of recent years that ensuring that the benefits of growth are widely shared and that the benefits translate into better education, health, and housing, then they will be able to manage the political changes with very positive outcomes. The key will be the demonstration by enlightened leaders that economic growth can bring substantive benefits to all members of society. A humanistic approach is both essential and probable.

Part III

Doing Business in the 21st Century

11

A Global State of Mind

> "To succeed in the boom requires a global state of mind."
>
> —George V. Grune,
> Chairman of The Reader's Digest Association, Inc.[1]

To succeed in the boom at the dawn of the 21st century, to maximize its benefits and contribute to its development, corporate leaders need to look at the world differently. We live in an increasingly integrated world economy full of opportunity, where "doing business" involves a myriad of new strategies and behaviors. It means having a vision about where the world is going and what your part in it will be. It means restructuring the company to make it genuinely multinational, being right on top of the latest global developments in your business sector, knowing what your competitors are doing, and having the right contacts. It also means establishing a reputation of excellence on a global level, a reputation that secures respect, and, in turn, an advantage among your peers, employees, customers, suppliers, and sources of finance. And, if you are a portfolio investor, rather than an entrepreneur or a corporate manager, then you will need to look to invest in companies that have all of these attributes.

In this chapter and the three that follow, we will discuss each of these attributes, offering examples of the successes and failures of many multinational companies. The fundamental components for winning in the new era are: having the right global attitude, recognizing the cultural challenges that the new Industrial Revolution poses to all enterprises, and fully understanding the concepts and the challenges of globalization.

We believe that truly being a successful global business requires more than having offices in several nations or selling product 9internationally. It is a mindset, an attitude that must pervade every part of a business.

George Grune not only articulated his concept of a global state of mind, but he positioned The Reader's Digest Association, Inc. accordingly. He continued the above-cited speech by saying:

> Of course a global strategy may not be right for every company. But it's interesting to note that almost all businesses that are global today—automobiles and consumer electronics, for example—were not always that way. Even if you work for a company with no global strategy, the shift in the business world to global marketing and positioning is so significant that it can't help but have an effect on you. I believe American companies are in a worldwide struggle for markets, both to defend positions at home and to seek new markets abroad. And that can be true even if you're planning to go into a small business.

> "Being a truly successful global business requires a mindset—an attitude that must pervade every part of the business."

Although he spoke with American business in mind, Grune's words of advice are just as applicable to most businesses in other nations. The global competition for markets has never been as intense as it is today, and it will become far more intense in the years ahead. The brass ring? New market opportunities.

The Reader's Digest Association, Inc. is an example of a company that has embraced a global vision for itself. Although the company has been involved in international business since 1938, it has only recently adopted a truly global perspective, an outlook that has created new corporate vigor and, concomitantly, new business growth. Indeed, the first paragraph of the corporation's 1992 Annual Report summed it up best. It said: "We are a successful global company driven by a strategic plan."

The company's best known product, *Reader's Digest* magazine, has a worldwide circulation of 27 million in 47 editions produced in 18 languages. The company's book sales in 1994, for example, were 56 million in 31 countries in 12 languages. It also sold 9 million units of its music collections in 20 countries and 4 million home video packages in 17 countries. Thinking globally, Grune saw the new opportunities for his enterprise. For example, the moment communism collapsed in Central and Eastern Europe, local language editions of the magazine were swiftly developed, providing the leading edge of corporate expansion there. Having a global state of mind is crucial to success in the era of the new Industrial Revolution, where the greatest growth will be outside of the traditional industrial economies.

Going Global

Traditionally, many corporations have considered their international business as subordinate to their domestic operations. Real priority to foreign business was rarely assigned, even when management recognized its potential. Many corporations remain in this "foreign business as secondary" mode; however, increasing numbers of businesses now understand that attention must be paid to the international arena, especially to the emerging markets, if continued growth is to be secured.

Whirlpool offers a good example. With $7 billion in annual sales of washers, dryers, and refrigerators and more than a 30 percent share of the U.S. market, Whirlpool has enjoyed great success. The trouble is that almost all households in the U.S. have such appliances and, although people trade up and buy replacement products, it no longer represents a market with growth potential.

The only way for Whirlpool to continue significant growth is by establishing itself outside of its home country. The company actually started business in Latin America as early as 1957, and, in the last decade, it has built a strong position for itself in Europe through acquisition. Now the focus is on Asia, where it predicts an annual sales growth of its products of between 8 and 12 percent for many years to come. As the company states: "Our success as a global company rests on our ability to position Whirlpool in Asia."[2]

Can a U.S. company in the appliances business take on the Japanese and Asians in their own part of the globe? Why not? Part of Whirlpool's strategy is to win a reputation for making quality products by demonstrating that it can make better products than its local rivals. It is achieving this by applying outstanding U.S. technology and management approaches to local skills in the new markets it is entering. This effort demanded substantial organizational talent. Whirlpool searched for talented individuals with meaningful experience and made a major effort to understand the dynamics of the region. This, in turn, led to decisions to establish an Asian headquarters in Tokyo, a design center in Singapore, and a key regional office in Hong Kong. The company then formed a joint venture with a Taiwan-based distributor and forged licensing agreements for manufacturing in China. A critical element in Whirlpool's game plan is building five manufacturing plants in Asia before the end of this decade.

> "In addition to thinking globally, companies must also keenly tailor approaches to local needs."

Whirlpool has a vision of its future as a global enterprise, and it is investing for the long-term to make this vision a profitable reality.

The Whirlpool example, one which is being increasingly replicated, is instructive for many corporate managements, but it also has a wider economic significance. That is, as increasing numbers of companies expand within the emerging markets and transfer knowledge to those areas, they contribute to the rapid development of middle-classes in those economies. The greater the transfer of capital and knowledge by the multi-national enterprises, as they adopt a global state of mind and see the full scope of new opportunities, the more they contribute to broad economic growth—to the building of the new Industrial Revolution.

Acting Local

A critical perspective pursued by the Reader's Digest Association, Inc., and common to an increasing number of other firms is that, while companies must think globally and evolve global strategies, they must also keenly tailor approaches to local needs. Reader's Digest Association, Inc., has seen the massive consumer market that is evolving across the world, and it applies the "plan globally, act locally" approach to the dozens of countries in which it now has offices.

Knowing local markets is imperative. We will stress this point over and over again, because, as Grune noted in his 1989 speech:

> Horror stories abound about companies that thought the world had become so homogenized that they could sell standardized products the same way everywhere. But the French don't drink orange juice for breakfast; Middle Easterners prefer toothpaste that tastes spicy; Japanese like herbs in their medicines; and some Mexicans use laundry detergent to wash dishes.

Just as rising consumer demands and growing infrastructure needs are attracting multinational corporations, so are new privatization policies. The combination of these factors is creating an explosion in the number of multinational enterprises. As we have noted earlier, there are now approximately 37,000 multinational corporations with over 170,000 foreign affiliates generating over $4.8 trillion in annual sales. These companies already directly employ about 73 million people, representing nearly 10 percent of paid employment in nonagricultural activities worldwide and close to 20 percent in developed countries alone. As many multinationals are responsible for vast numbers of employees through their contracting operations, these corporations could be indirectly influencing the lives of over 150 million workers. For example, NIKE employs a core staff of only 9,000 people, but through subcontracting it employs an additional 75,000 people outside of the United States.[3]

The Global Mentality

The pressures of the world's marketplace are forcing cross-border mergers, new international joint ventures, and the creation of new multinationals.

Gerber has long been the leading baby food manufacturer in the United States, a success most might consider satisfying. But Gerber looked global, and that opened the way for its acquisition in 1994 by Switzerland's Sandoz pharmaceutical company for $3.7 billion. Gerber had seen the attractions of the international market and had sought, at considerable expense, to develop foreign sales. At the time of the Sandoz deal, international sales represented just over 15 percent of its $1.3 billion total sales. Gerber knew that to achieve greater growth it needed an alliance with a company that was familiar with the multinational business landscape and was positioned for substantial expansion in scores of markets. Gerber also knew that going global demanded international know-how and confidence, capital, and a distribution system—all assets it lacked, but that Sandoz had. In short, the alliance was forged by a shrinking world, where success, even in the single richest national market in the world, is just no longer good enough.[4]

The pressures of multinationalism are increasing. Even AT&T, the most domestic of U.S. companies, has changed its name and its business strategy because, as it stated in its 1993 Annual Report, "We learned that meeting customer needs in a world where companies do business around the globe required us to become a global company."

AT&T's largest U.S. customers were rapidly becoming global multinationals, and the communications company had the choice of either striving to continue to be relevant to these customer needs or losing its clients to aggressive foreign and domestic rivals with world views and world organizations. To assist it in creating a global image, AT&T dropped the "American" in its official name in 1994. As such, AT&T is no longer an acronym for American Telephone and Telegraph Company; it is now the official name. Underscoring its new, worldly perspective, AT&T also renamed its NCR unit, which is now known as AT&T Global Information and Solutions.

AT&T is finding that the competition in its domestic U.S. market is becoming tougher, as European and Japanese firms seek to forge strategic alliances with AT&T's U.S. rivals. Those alliances, between British Telecom and MCI and between many other vendors, will also influence the global strategies of AT&T's competitors and pose major threats to AT&T outside America. All the same, the adoption of a 'global state of mind' is difficult for a corporation which still does the overwhelming amount of its business in its traditional home market and whose management is filled with people whose whole experience has been in the United States.

In 1994, an AT&T publication for its 300,000 corporate employees used a gorilla to symbolize the people of Africa. The story made the front pages of newspapers around the globe, embarrassing AT&T,

and the company swiftly made public apologies. Management mistakes were made that allowed low-level staff and outside consultants to produce such a gaffe and create an image of an insensitive company. This admittedly extreme incident illustrates the complexity of fundamentally changing corporate culture in traditional corporations that must go global and demonstrate acute international cultural sensitivity.

The difficulties at AT&T of genuinely thinking global were highlighted, for example, at a mid-1993 symposium that the corporation organized for its international managers. The fact that the symposium was staged and that excellent international experts were asked to participate highlighted AT&T's earnest desire to strengthen the international information base of its managers. However, the continuing mindset that the world and employees are divided into American and foreign was all too evident in some of the presentations by corporate executives, who repeatedly talked about hiring "foreign nationals" as if these would be some form of second-class employees.

AT&T is not the only telecom giant that is moving somewhat ponderously towards becoming global. Many telecom companies around the world are still in the public sector, or have been recently privatized, and they all need to learn about global competition at great speed. Each of them face new competitors who are fit, fast, flexible, and far more advanced in striving to understand the world and its new opportunities—namely companies in the engineering, electronics, computer, and cellular telephone fields, all of whom see enormous Third World market opportunities in telecommunications.

Companies like AT&T, who look at the global stage and know they must soon join it, must also recognize how far behind they already are in the competitive global arena. An example of one of the frontrunners is Asea Brown Boveri (ABB), the Swedish–Swiss international engineering group. ABB not only operates in 140 countries, it also has core product development and manufacturing in at least a dozen countries, and its ownership and management are increasingly international. In addition, ABB has a perspective on its corporate culture that makes it the model multinational corporation—the type of enterprise that will be constantly used as an exemplar when comparing the degree to which giant corporations have moved from essentially national thinking to multinational.

ABB is among Europe's most respected multinationals, due in no small measure to the degree to which it has implemented global management approaches. In early 1994, ABB's chief executive, Percy Barnevik, wrote in Britain's *Financial Times* about the need to build multinational teams. He stated:

> As business gets more globalized, the competitive advantages of multinational teams increase. Any single-nationality corporate culture will run into problems as soon as it aims to integrate larger operations from other countries. At the same time, we strive to develop a global corporate culture for all members of our multinational teams. One key element is having a common language. English was chosen at the outset, although a minority of the present 218,000 employees have English as their mother language. Today, all executives use English as their common language, and ABB's currency for global reporting and consolidation is the U.S. dollar. Most importantly, from the very beginning, ABB established a common set of values, policies, and operational guidelines to safeguard and promote a group-wide, umbrella culture.

> "As business gets more globalized, the competitive advantages of multinational teams increase."

Companies that are already fully global in the ABB sense, or are moving rapidly in this direction, are being recognized by their peers and by investors. Additionally, Third World governments are making particular efforts to attract these firms to invest in their countries. The advantages of being seen as genuinely global and effective on the world stage are substantial.

What constitutes "most respected"? In June 1994, the *Financial Times*, together with the Price Waterhouse auditing firm, asked that question of 637 top executives from Europe's largest companies. Some of the results of this survey are shown in the table below. As you can see, what won accolades for these companies was their skill to secure exceptional customer loyalty, to demostrate the quality of their employees, and to solve problems and provide benefits to their customers in many different national markets. In each case, the leading companies were seen as attaining records of long-term growth and profitability under firm and creative

management. Each of the companies was seen as having clear policies and objectives. It is the combination of factors like these, trans-
lated to the global arena, that is bringing success to modern
multinationals today.[5]

The survey also showed that the companies seen by their
peers across Europe as being the most respected included BMW,
Deutsche Bank, Möet Hennesy Louis Vuitton, Ciba-Geigy, Siemens,
Unilever, Reuters, Royal Dutch Shell, Marks and Spencer, British
Telecom, British Airways, and ABB.

**QUALITIES THAT DETERMINE THE MOST RESPECTED
CORPORATIONS (Survey of leading European firms by *Financial
Times*/Price Waterhouse)**

Issue	Most Important	Least Important
Customer Focus	Enjoys high customer loyalty	Makes good use of technology in its customer services
People	People have the means and the facilities to deliver results	Has demonstrated "real" equal opportunities
Products and Services	Products solve problems and provide benefits	Invests heavily in research and development
Business Performance	Has shown consistent growth and long-term profitability	Is a low-cost producer
Leadership and Management	Displays positive management style and attractive behavior	Takes a strong position on social issues
Strategy	Clear policy and objectives	Focusing upon revenue growth rather than cost reduction
Environment	Invests in pollution reduction measures	Policy shows in products and packaging

Companies that win respect and move ahead with great skill and speed into the fastest growing economies in the world will be the winners in the years immediately ahead and on into the new century. They will be the companies that clearly and fully recognize the extraordinary business opportunities that already exist and that are rapidly being created.

12

A World of New Business Opportunities

Business opportunities are opening at a fierce pace, but competition to win these opportunities is just as fierce. To truly succeed, you must be proactive, be swift to go for new ventures, and have the skill to close deals fast. Some of the greatest opportunities, particularly attractive to the largest multinational corporations, are emerging in the infrastructure arena. Some are absolutely new projects, while others involve privatizations.

AT&T has been scrambling to be a player. Its perspectives and management may still be rather provincial, but it is acutely

> "To succeed in the fiercely competitive global marketplace, you will need to be proactive, swift, and have the skills to close deals fast."

aware of just where the big growth will be in its business sector. AT&T's 1993 Annual Report notes that:

> China wants to increase phone service twenty-fold by 2020. That means 15 to 17 million lines must be installed annually over the next 27 years. In helping that country reach its goals, AT&T will become China's largest telecommunications supplier. And the work there could be the most extensive international project in our history.[1]

In fact, there is such an urgency on the part of the Chinese in the telecommunications sector that it is questionable whether AT&T can move fast enough to position itself for maximum effect. The

Chinese want to quadruple the number of phone lines in the country to around 100 million in the final five years of this century. The only way to achieve this, they decided, is to use the private sector. As a result, a minimum of three rival companies will be established in China under the regulation of the Ministry of Posts and Telecommunications (MPT). Nynex and Bell South, also from the United States, have been very active in China and seem determined to give AT&T a run for its money in this market.[2]

More generally, the infrastructure data on the Third World highlights not only the progress that developing countries have made, but also the huge needs that remain to be filled. Those needs, of course, represent opportunities for Western firms with capital, technology, and management know-how. Huge areas of potential growth can be found across the infrastructure board, from roads, transportation, electricity, and sanitation to telecommunications.

In terms of electricity production, for example, Ghana produced just 374 million kilowatt hours in 1960, while 30 years later the volume was 5.4 billion kw hours; Brazil increased its output tenfold in 30 years to reach 222 billion kw hours in 1990. As for sanitation infrastructure, while it is true that tiny Benin in Africa managed to boost access to sanitation from 14 percent of its population to 45 percent over the last 20 years, that still means the majority of its people lack such essential needs. In Bolivia, where access to sanitation rose from 13 percent of the population to 26 percent by 1990, that means almost three-quarters of the population still has a desperate need that will demand large, national investments.

> ## "Two-thirds of all the people in the world have never made a telephone call!"

Finally, in the telecom business, the incentive is simple to understand: two-thirds of all the people in the world have never made a telephone call! Privatization has made it possible for AT&T and its rivals to seek to exploit this opportunity. After all, the coming decade may see greater outlays on global telecommunications than all that has been spent in the United States in the last 150 years.

David Frost, a senior executive at Bell Atlantic International, Inc., noted at an AT&T management seminar in mid-1993 that:[3]

> There are now more than 50 privatizations underway or under study around the world in the telecommunications sector. That number is growing monthly. A number of them have already been completed, with six of them—Argentina, Chile, Hong Kong, Mexico, New Zealand, Venezuela—involving strategic foreign investors. . . As a result of these six privatizations, more than 17 million access lines have moved into private hands. The *Financial Times* estimates that privatizations involving 95 million additional telephone lines are likely to be completed over the next few years.

TELEPHONE MAIN LINES (number of connections)
Examples from the world's most populated
developing countries

Country (million)	Population (million)	Total lines in 1975 (million)	Total lines in 1990
China	1,162	3.3	6.8
India	883	1.5	5.0
Indonesia	184	0.2	1.1
Brazil	154	2.5	9.4
Pakistan	119	0.2	0.8

By comparison, the population to telephone line equation in the most developed countries is (numbers in millions) as follows and has not significantly changed over the last 20 years:

U.S.	255	136
U.K.	58	25
Japan	124	55
Germany	81	30
France	57	28

For many of the largest foreign direct investors, privatizations are going to be the prime channel into the hearts of many developing economies. As the International Finance Corporation (IFC) has noted:

> Between 1988 and 1992, governments in developing countries realized more than $60 billion in revenues from the sale of state-owned assets. Most privatizations have occurred in Latin America, but the

trend is visible throughout the developing world—the Czech Republic, Hungary, Malaysia, Philippines, Poland, Portugal, and Thailand are just a few of the countries that have made significant progress in this area.[4]

In addition to infrastructure improvements, privatizations are also proving important to the building of capital markets and stock exchanges in developing countries. The listing of shares in the largest enterprises in the country provides depth and strength to emerging stock exchanges. And, as discussed in Chapter Two, the establishment of increasingly sophisticated, formal capital markets provides many local citizens in these countries with excellent opportunities to convert resources gained from informal economic activity into the formal economy.

The speed with which privatization has moved ahead has much to do with the swiftness of some of the leading international service companies, that is, the major brokerage houses, investment banks, and accounting firms. They all saw vast new markets for themselves in the arena of privatization. They saw themselves taking the lead in restructuring publicly-owned corporations from Buenos Aires to Budapest—and making huge fees in the process.

Thousands of privatizations have already brought tens of billions of dollars into the coffers of developing countries, and the 1995-2000 period will only see a further explosion of privatizations, with many new and unique opportunities for foreign direct investors. As stories of the opportunities proliferate, competition is bound to increase.

The largest and most successful privatization program of recent years took place in Germany. Following the reunification of eastern and western parts of the country in 1991, the Treuhandanstalt Corporation was established to privatize more than 2,500 East German enterprises. It sold them off or liquidated them at a rapid pace. Many of the enterprises were given to the company employees and managers and may very well fail; it will take years before an objective evaluation can be made of the effectiveness of the Treuhandanstalt's approach. Nonetheless, the key objective was attained: Almost all of the enterprises held by the State were moved off the public sector's books. These developments have contributed to making eastern Germany the fastest growing region of economic expansion in Europe today.

Privatization has been the most stunning aspect of economic reform and change in the former Soviet Union. Vast numbers of enterprises have been moved from governmental control, and, by mid-1995, fully 40 percent of national output was accounted for by the private sector. In the Czech Republic, the scale of privatization has been even greater, and today the private sector (which did not exist at all five years ago) now accounts for 80 percent of the country's production of goods and services.

If one is willing to take the risk, vast numbers of inexpensive enterprises are available, many of which have within them the potential for significant success under efficient management. This is true for public sector enterprises now being set for privatization in Pakistan, Egypt, Turkey, Vietnam, many African countries, as well as throughout Latin America. An example of a recent success is illustrated in Enron's investment in Argentina.

When Argentina's gas industry was put up for privatization in 1992, Enron Corporation of Texas paid $140 million for a 17.5 percent interest in one of its pipelines, Transportadora de Gas del Sur. Enron has already secured multimillion dollar dividends from this investment, and the value of its original investment, based on stock market quotations, more than doubled in 24 months. Enron brought to Argentina several assets that won it such a bargain: capital, technology, managerial know-how, and a global perspective. The latter factor is seen as crucial by emerging economies—the best foreign multinational companies bring access to global markets, abundant foreign partners, foreign customers and suppliers, and approaches to doing business that draw from the success stories learned in the international arena.

Using Rising Skill Levels

The privatization path is important for some multinational corporations, but there are other opportunities availing themselves on an unprecedented scale. For instance, skill levels are increasing in low-income countries, yet labor costs still remain far less than in the most advanced industrial countries. This scenario is creating exceptional opportunities. Although labor costs in these countries will rise fast, many current situations appear to offer the type of long-term comparative advantage for which a growing number of multinational corporations are now zealously searching. The high-tech boom in India is an example.

The *World Investment Report 1993*, produced by UNCTAD, illustrates the key points:

> The tendency for companies to put high-value functions in places where the best and cheapest production capabilities exist is illustrated by the number of computer and software foreign affiliates (of multinational corporations) that are located in India, many of them in Bangalore. Through wholly owned export operations or joint ventures, Texas Instruments Inc., Motorola Inc., Hewlett-Packard Co., Apple Computer Inc., Sun Microsystems Inc., and Intel Corporation have all set up operations there. Dell Computer Corporation is planning to establish a plant to manufacture computer motherboards for export, and IBM has formed a joint venture with India's biggest industrial firm, the Tata Group.

In another example, in early 1993 Swissair began transferring its revenue accounting office to Bombay. It established an Indian affiliate for this purpose and took 75 percent of the shares, with Tata Consulting Services (TCS) of Bombay taking the remaining 25 percent stake. The massive computerization undertaken for this process has enabled the centralization of a function once done in dozens of national locations, with substantial cost savings for the Swiss company. The extent to which global thinking companies are taking the fullest advantage of industrialization in the developing world today suggests far, far more of this activity will be seen in the period ahead.

Trade Expands Opportunities

Finally, the scope of opportunities for global business is being broadened almost daily by trade policy developments. At the most general level, global trade liberalization actions are being stimulated by the World Trade Organization in Geneva. This new body is the result of the seven-year-long Uruguay Round of trade negotiations involving more than 100 countries that concluded in 1994 with agreements to significantly reduce many barriers to free trade and to create rules and approaches that will stimulate a global, open trade regime.

Global commerce is also being boosted by agreements at the regional level. A recent example of regional trade liberalization is the North American Free Trade Agreement (NAFTA) between Canada, the U.S., and Mexico. In time, if Latin Americans have their say, NAFTA will also expand southwards, eventually encompassing all of the Americas. In addition to NAFTA, several other regional trade agreements are facilitating trade growth around the globe. The largest of the regional

> "The scope of opportunities for global business is broadened almost daily by trade policy developments."

trade bloc arrangements embraces the 15 member countries of the European Union and will in time expand to embrace parts of Eastern Europe. Almost each week, new agreements are being forged within other regional trade blocs. Among these are: ASEAN (Association of South East Asian Nations), CACM (Central American Common Market), LAFTA/LAIA (Latin American Free Trade Area/Latin American Integration Association), ECOWAS (Economics Community of West African States), PTA (Preferential Trade Area for Eastern and Southern Africa), and SADC (Southern African Development Community).

The next tier of cooperation consists of bilateral trade agreements within distinct regions. No part of the globe is seeing more activity in this context now than the Americas, stimulated in part by the NAFTA deals and in part by the resurgence of economic growth in Latin America. Each week, new bilateral trade treaties are being signed in Latin America and new talks of regional integration are being held. U.S. exports alone to Latin America doubled between 1986 and 1993 to total $80 billion. Growth in exports stimulated by bilateral liberalization agreements in Latin America have been staggering. For example, in 1992 the annual export growth rate between Argentina and Brazil was 59 percent, 51 percent between Argentina and Paraguay, 45 percent between Chile and Mexico, 47 percent between Colombia and Venezuela, and 34 percent between Argentina and Uruguay. Many Latin countries have cut their import tariffs in half in the last decade, and further major cuts are projected.

The rapidly changing, integrated global economy will grow even more quickly as business adapts. Never before have the opportunities been as large on a global scale. There is no compelling reason to suggest that they will not be even bigger tomorrow than they are today. The key to reaping the benefits of these opportunities is seeing very clearly the shape of things to come and then conceptualizing how you can best take advantage of the emerging boom.

13

Globalization

We have no doubt that the great corporate profits in the future will come from global business. There will be a boom. While there are risks to the smooth evolution of an Industrial Revolution in all parts of the Third World and Central and Eastern Europe, we are confident that most countries will enjoy unprecedented prosperity. But we are concerned that this exceptionally bright prospect will lull investors, entrepreneurs, and managers into underestimating the complexities of the world's business landscape.

In the chapters ahead, we will look at many facets of the managerial challenge, stressing the need for a clear vision, the dangers of overconfidence, and the vital need to redefine the corporation in order to fully meet the challenges of the new era. In this chapter, we underscore the meaning of globalization and illustrate our points by providing examples from some world giants—J.P. Morgan, Ford, and Volkswagen.

> "Global presence is not a choice, but a strategic imperative for all growing, high-performance companies."
>
> —The Conference Board, New York.[1]

In 1994, the Conference Board of New York surveyed[2] 1,250 publicly-traded U.S. manufacturers to understand more about globalization trends. Of the firms surveyed, 92.5 percent reported direct foreign investment, foreign sales, or other forms of international activity. The Conference Board's conclusion was that the internationalization of marketing and manufacturing activity has become irreversible, even for relatively small companies. The survey suggested that profitability rises in firms with a broad global scope.

The Conference Board noted that the typical path of corporate development is to undertake international roll-outs in several stages, moving from development of exports and sales infrastructure abroad to eventual production overseas. However, its study of smaller multinationals indicated that there may be an alternative approach. By advancing to multinational engagement well before the milestone of $1 billion in annual sales, a firm may compress, or even leapfrog, the intervening stages. Not only is size no obstacle to international expansion, but early entry into the global market may be a clear sign of success.

The most telling conclusion of all from the survey was simply that developing markets present a growing strategic challenge. As tariff and regulatory barriers fall and these markets become more competitive, U.S. multinationals will increasingly consolidate offshore production in order to achieve economies of scale. The Conference Board noted that all U.S. manufacturers will face the challenge of raising profitability in a world where it is increasingly difficult to find markets where they enjoy a clear-cut competitive advantage.

J.P. Morgan's Way

The challenge is by no means confined to manufacturers. Service companies are going to be just as hard-pressed in a more competitive global environment, and they will have to be just as visionary in their global strategies as manufacturers. The approaches taken by one of America's oldest banking houses is instructive in understanding some of the new, necessary approaches to globalization. J.P. Morgan has been involved in international finance on a continuous basis for longer than any other U.S. bank. Over the last dozen years, under the leadership of Lewis Preston, Dennis Weatherstone, and the current Chairman, Douglas A. Warren III, the finance house displayed the wisdom of never taking its knowledge of the world for granted or believing that any of its clients will be loyal to the bank for old time's sake.

J.P. Morgan, whose multicultural and multinational top management team reflects the universe in which it operates (for example, its chairman and chief executive officer until early 1995 was British-born and a diversity of nationalities occupy the top executive suites), constantly strengthens and secures its image in the countries where it operates by distributing brochures, often in local languages, underlining top management's international commitment.

Weatherstone, one of the outstanding bankers of his generation, saw clearly how firms had to deepen their international work and constantly explain what they were doing with singular clarity. Distributed with J.P. Morgan's 1992 and 1993 annual reports was a brochure on "Capability and character in global finance," in which Weatherstone declared:

> During the past decade, we have transformed J.P. Morgan to confront the new realities of global finance. We've drawn on commercial, investment, and merchant banking traditions to cast our firm in a new mold—one shaped by our clients' evolving needs and the world's evolving markets.[3]

J.P. Morgan reminds its international contacts that, in 1838, American businessman George Peabody opened a London merchant banking firm, establishing the roots of the House of Morgan. Today, few companies better understand positioning than J.P. Morgan, as it displays what it calls "business principles at work." It uses a distinctive vocabulary to define its business, as much for purposes of marketing clarity as for purposes of internal communication. The aim is to ensure that Morgan professionals around the globe reinforce key concepts and initiatives, share a common strategic perspective, and speak for the firm with a unified voice.

Rather than using a general term like contacts, J.P. Morgan emphasizes the importance of "enduring relationships," noting:

> We strive to build relationships of trust and discretion over the long term. And we focus on serving our clients' needs, not on doing deals. We always put our clients' interests first, and we are resolute in defending those interests.

Instead of the bland word knowledge, J.P. Morgan highlights "sound research," stressing:

Our strategic advice is based on comprehensive, fundamental research. Our analytical depth and commitment to objectivity ensure that our recommendations reflect the best available information and adhere to our clients' best interests.

In talking about positioning, J.P. Morgan stresses: "international presence," commenting:

Our perspective is truly global. Our international network of financial specialists provides expertise in, and access to, all major financial markets—not only in the industrially developed regions, but also in emerging economies of the world.

Such efforts as these highlight the J.P. Morgan commitment to being a global enterprise, and the constant reminder to staff and customers of this simple fact strengthens the basic, crucial attitudes that govern the business. J.P. Morgan no longer needs to structure itself for global business; it has already succeeded. Now, its challenge is to keep pace with global changes and constantly refine its approaches as global business becomes bigger and more complex.

VW and FORD : Contrasts in Globalization

Meanwhile, increasing numbers of manufacturing corporations in the United States, as well as in Western Europe and Japan, are now concluding that the path to big profits is global. The findings of the Conference Board survey highlight this critical fact. For a long time, some of the world's biggest corporations have put this finding at the center of their strategies. But, as the examples of Ford and VW show, there can be very different ways of going global.

Henry Ford II had a major influence over his company for two generations, and he argued repeatedly, even at times of great difficulty, that Ford's long-term success would come from being a world company. He made sure that Ford Motor Company constantly invested in building and refining a global empire. He constantly pushed to ensure that the diverse parts of the Ford network were increasingly integrated with each other and that people with a global market understanding were promoted.

The appointment of Alex Trotman to head Ford in the 1990s is the logical outcome of the Henry Ford II legacy. Trotman was born in England, raised in Scotland, educated at Michigan State University in the U.S., and has dual British and American citizenship. He has considerable work experience in both North America and Europe and the perfect profile and background to pursue Ford's global ambitions. He sees the world as a single market for Ford to capture. Trotman is the product of the Henry Ford II school to the degree that Ford warned against being complacent about the international arena. This ceaseless traveller understood, often more intuitively than from research, that the world market was changing very fast and that Ford would have to keep changing to keep current and win.

By contrast, the leadership of Volkswagen of Germany since 1970 has lacked a clear vision of the world market and has found it difficult to manage in a world of dynamic change. One result, for example, is that, in 1970, Volkswagen sold 569,182 new cars in the United States, and it sold less than 22,000 cars in 1993.[4]

In the 1950s, VW understood that its growth could be derived from the German domestic market alone and that it produced cars so different from those made in the U.S. by General Motors, Ford, and Chrysler that it could provide Americans with a real alternative. But VW let the U.S. and other foreign markets slip out of its grasp in the early 1970s, as it turned inwards, confronted a host of management and financial difficulties, and failed to create a new, global concept for a new era. VW never saw the Japanese coming.

In the early 1970s, VW was almost the only seller of small cars to Americans. As the Arab oil price hikes shook the global economy in late 1973 and 1974, manufacturers of automobiles had a unique opportunity to exploit the new fuel sensitivity of American consumers. VW should have enjoyed record sales, but, instead, it left the field open to the Japanese. In Tokyo, executives saw the long-term opportunities in North America, and they raced to invest on a huge scale to grasp a major share of the richest and largest national market in the world.

VW could not adapt to the new competition. It launched new operations, or expanded operations, in a number of markets, but time and again it failed to recognize the political and economic trends that were shaping business opportunities and the skills of its competitors. For example, in the late 1970s and early 1980s it expanded production rapidly in Latin America, failing to see the mounting debt burdens that the countries of the region were amassing and the prospect of an era of recession in that part of the world. In the United States, to take another example, VW invested in a production plant in Pennsylvania, but failed to produce models that had strong appeal to American consumers. In an era where Ford Motor Company was creating new model revolutions and changing public tastes with its Taurus models, VW was still offering yesterday's cars.

VW has struggled for almost a quarter century to find a new global vision and the mixture of skills and talents to win in the international market. In the last couple of years, it has gone through a full-scale overhaul of internal management, hired new top managers, and sought to redefine itself for the 21st century. It remains to be seen whether VW can succeed.

Meanwhile, Ford has built an international management leadership team to undertake one of the most ambitious strategies in modern manufacturing—the creation of world cars, built, assembled, and sold in scores of national markets through a highly integrated set of Ford management systems. The Ford Contour went on sale in the United States in late 1994 with a sticker price of less than $14,000 and the intense hopes of Alex Trotman that it would do just as well in North America as it did in 1993 and 1994 in Europe, where, under the name of the Ford Mondeo, it outsold all of the rivals in its class. As the name Mondeo indicates, this is a world car. Never before has a single manufacturer produced a motor car for the global market in such volume and with the involvement of production and assembly plants scattered in many countries.

The world car venture cost Ford over $6 billion in investment, and, if the market responds well, Ford has the global capacity to produce 800,000 units of this car (or versions of it) per year around the globe. With the $6 billion, Ford has purchased three basic, related models, two new engines, and two new gear boxes, not to mention its new and sophisticated global production, assembly, and marketing network. The Mondeo project is reflective of something far larger for Ford—a global strategy that dwarfs anything that it has attempted in the past. The company has merged North American and European managements, charting the way for the full integration of design, development, production, and marketing on a global scale. This is a complex task, but the fact is that the only way to build the financial muscle to support attacks on the rapidly emerging economies, which offer immense growth potential, is by taking maximum advantage of new technologies to secure global economies of scale. The prime, long-term focus is on Asia—especially China and India, but also Indonesia, Thailand, and Vietnam—and on South America.

Ford is demonstrating that the integration of today's multipolar world is already so substantial that the translation of a global state of mind into tens of thousands of micro-management decisions, involving scores of countries, may yield vast rewards. To make automobile parts in dozens of factories in different countries, ship them overseas to central assembly plants, and then ship them across national borders again to be sold in foreign markets, involves incredible organization. Only in an age of sophisticated information technology, high levels of skilled workers in many countries, and highly experienced international managers can such a strategy even be attempted. Ford is setting a new standard in globalization.

"I have envisaged Ford with a global organization since the late 1960s. Its natural evolution," Trotman told *The Economist* magazine in July 1994, adding," Now is the right time for such a change. The tools are there—computers and communications—and we have a strong balance sheet."

The Mondeo is no more than a first step. Despite the claims to be global, the integration achieved by early 1995 did not, for example, include Jaguar in Britain, Ford's top-of-the-line, prestige subsidiary, or Ford's 25 percent stake in Mazda in Japan. Both of these important parts of Ford will become integrated in the Ford global model line within a few years. The Ford Escort has been the mainstay of the Ford range in Europe for years, and Trotman, who these days appears to give endless interviews to promote his global image, told the *Financial Times* in April 1994, "The next generation (of the Escort) might mean that we have one development for Ford and Mazda worldwide."

Former Ford Chairman Philip Caldwell, also involved in Trotman's media offensive, noted to *Forbes* magazine in June 1994:

> Fifty percent to 60 percent of the world's population is not being served by the Ford Motor Co. If we go about as we have in the past, the economics won't leave much left over for pursuit of these new market opportunities."

This comment hints at the most compelling reason for Ford's actions to globalize management and production as fast as possible—competition and the demands of a fast-changing, global automobile industry. Ford might be ahead of its rivals in globalization, but the others may find they have no alternative but to follow Ford's approach. The rapid changes in the structure of the global economy are demanding rapid responses from even the largest enterprises.

Japanese companies now have 11 assembly plants and three engine plants in North America, in a combined industry that now dwarfs, for example, the total car industries of Britain, Italy, and Spain. Honda is the largest North American car producer to export to Japan. As BMW bought Rover in Britain, the Japanese built a huge North American presence, Mercedes opened a U.S. assembly plant, and every motor manufacturer sought to rationalize output systems. The compelling focus for all is on the prize in the 21st century, which Trotman has simply stated as the fact that today 80 percent of the world's population accounts for only 8 percent of global automobile sales. This will change and everyone in the industry knows it.

The competition, among the leading car makers to rapidly build a strong presences in Asia is intense, and it will become still hotter. The way ahead for the Chinese is by developing joint ventures with foreign corporations who are willing to build full production plants in the country. DRI McGraw-Hill, quoted in the *Financial Times* in October 1994, forecast that sales of automobiles in China by the end of this decade will be around one million units per year, compared to 430,000 in 1993 and only 78,000 in 1990.

Model Globalization

In the arena of manufacturing today, Ford can serve as an outstanding example of a company that understands globalization and the exciting global business prospects ahead. Ford is among the ten largest multinational corporations in the world. It has been in the business of globalization longer than almost any other major enterprise, and it has long understood that it must have a world vision backed with a mindset that makes no distinctions between staff, plant locations, or business partners, on the basis of nationality, color, or creed.

The global environment has become more hospitable to the multinational corporation, and the prospects for far larger and still more profitable global business ventures are expanding. We believe corporate leaders must think, act, and organize globally, hiring the best international talent, delegating to foreign nationals, building strong partnerships around the world with non-American firms, and demonstrating over and over again an awareness of a changing market. They must start with a clear vision of the world's rapidly evolving markets and where their corporations need to be in order to maximize the boom opportunities. We believe that portfolio investors, in analyzing corporations, need to pay close attention to the articulation of such visions and to the awareness by corporate leaders of the profits to be won through globalization.

14

Entrepreneurial Vision

oyal Dutch Shell, Exxon, IBM, General Motors, and Hitachi are the world's five largest multinational enterprises. Between them, in the early 1990s, they had total global assets of around $550 billion, global sales of around $460 billion, and they directly employed approximately 1.6 million people worldwide. These companies, together with a few dozen other large corporations, wield exceptional power, particularly in the emerging economies. They have the ability to reallocate business between countries, to open and close factories, introduce new technologies, and purchase scores of enterprises. In spite of their past successes, however, some of these giants will become complacent in an increasingly competitive world and will slip from their leadership positions. Others are so bureaucratic that they will find it intensely difficult to define their approaches to meet the challenges of a far more integrated world economy. They too will slip from the top echelons.

Their successors, meanwhile, will rise from the middle ranks, proving to be more creative, flexible, and adaptable. They will be the new leaders. The corporations most likely to succeed, to reshape international business and profit by it, will be those that have a distinct vision of their futures. We will discuss the specifics of establishing goals and redefining a business in coming chapters. First, we need to take a step back and talk about vision—because you cannot redefine what you cannot see.

When it comes to setting a vision in international business, few entrepreneurs in this century have been quite as extraordinary as Dr. Armand Hammer, the former chairman and CEO of Occidental Petroleum. Dr. Hammer built a host of international businesses, and he embraced Eastern Europe 70 years before it became fashionable, completing some of his first business deals with Lenin.

Dr. Hammer demonstrated that, as long as every aspect of the game plan was well defined and executed, profits could be turned by doing the opposite of what was fashionable. Nobody wanted to trade with Lenin's new communist nation, except a young doctor from New York who would eventually have a hand in almost every major West–East deal. Hammer always had a precise vision of where he was going and what he aimed to achieve.

Armand Hammer grew up in New York and studied medicine, but he never practiced. Back in 1920, upon graduation, he decided the world had to learn to work with the new, communist Russia. His vision was seeing business opportunities in a country whose ideology was anti-private enterprise. He saw the evolution of West–East trade on a major scale. Dr. Hammer held true to his vision until his death just a few years ago. In his Los Angeles office, he proudly displayed photographs of himself with Lenin, Stalin, and every subsequent Russian leader, as well as every American President since Hoover. He had confidence in his vision, and he worked to acquire the knowledge and the contacts that enabled him to position himself to maximize opportunities. The importance of doing comprehensive research and securing first-class contacts are subjects we will deal with in later chapters in this book; they are crucial to the implementation of a global business vision.

> "Articulating a vision for the coming boom is a daunting challenge to corporate leadership."

We cannot stress how vital a clear vision is to the success of businesses in the new Industrial Revolution. Put simply, companies that do not know where they are going in this rapidly changing global economy will be left behind. Although articulating a vision for the first decades of the 21st century is a daunting challenge to corporate leadership, it is the first step in the process of going global. The best way to talk about vision is to illustrate what it can do. Here are some examples.

Reuters Sees Far Ahead

Few companies have been more successful in translating rapid developments in the integration of the world of finance into handsome profits than Reuters Holdings PLC, the U.K.-based international news and information organization. Much of this success is due to men who saw that the world's capital markets were moving toward a single, 24-hour global market years before the term globalization became fashionable. Specifically, it was the entrepreneurial vision of Michael Nelson which took an essentially obscure news information service, transformed it into one of the most admired companies in the world, and, in the process, changed the face and tempo of global financial markets.

In the mid-1960s, Reuters was a stuffy enterprise owned by a group of newspapers in the U.K., Australia, and New Zealand. It had a great history, but few imagined it would have a greater future. In fact, at the dawn of the computer age in international financial communications, Reuters was still widely thought of as the news service that relied on pigeons.

At that time, however, Nelson lost a power struggle at Reuters and was put in charge of what then was seen as a dumping ground in the firm—the economic news service department. He had aspired to be the Managing Director and run the general news service, sending reporters across the world to be the first to report wars, elections, and great sporting events. Instead, Nelson became the Deputy Managing Director (a position he was to hold for a quarter of a century until his retirement) and ran a department that churned out weekly, duplicated reports on sugar, coffee, and cocoa markets, reporting financial market price changes through clattering telex machines hidden in dusty corners of the offices of brokers and bankers. This was not the glamour side of journalism.

Nonetheless, Nelson took his charge seriously. He understood that the coming years would see an explosion in international finance and that Reuters could be at the heart of this development. He understood that investors, banks, and all manner of financial institutions would increasingly trade across national borders and need market information from around the globe. Soon after he took charge of the economics section, in the mid-1960s, Reuters began hooking up stock markets around the world to the offices of stock brokers in London and New York through leased telecommunications systems and primitive computers. The concept was established.

Continuous innovation and investment in technologies made Reuters' economic and financial services essential for everyone trading in international markets, from Singapore to Sweden. As the Reuters systems improved, the volume of world trade in financial instruments increased. As the volume of trading rose, the demands for Reuters products grew. In 1984, 20 years after making its first, tentative step into electronic international transmission of financial data, Reuters was floated as a public company. Today, it is a global leader in its field, with a reputation as an outstandingly managed, dynamic corporation, spanning every segment of the world's rapidly growing financial markets.[1]

WPP Group plc

Earlier in this book, we noted Martin Sorrell's vision and its pay-off as IBM selected WPP's Ogilvy and Mather subsidiary for its global account. Let us look more closely at how one person's global vision can create a vast corporation and drive it to success.

WPP became the first fully global marketing services company (embracing research, advertising, public relations, business design, and other allied services) because one man recognized that, in the era of the new Industrial Revolution, increasing numbers of multinational enterprises would seek to implement marketing concepts on a fully global basis. Naturally, Sorrell realized, they want to hire consultants and agencies that think as globally as they do.

Born in the U.K. and educated in the U.K. and at the Harvard Business School, Sorrell was fascinated by the international business world. Advertising and finance proved to be his vehicles, but he also understood that building something big demanded an equally big vision that spread well beyond the borders of the United Kingdom. By the time he was in his mid-thirties, he was viewed as a financial wizard in London's conservative banking circles. He was already chief financial officer of Saatchi & Saatchi, widely considered to be among the most creative and fastest growing advertising companies in the world at that time. But Sorrell was keen to move from behind the shadows of the Saatchi brothers to center stage. Bankers were ready to back his vision of creating the first major multinational marketing services company in the world. By 1995, as WPP entered its tenth year, it was the world's largest marketing services company, with global revenues in excess of $2.5 billion.

Sorrell achieved his goal in under five years. In the mid-1980s, with backing from the banking fraternity, he took an obscure London Stock Exchange-listed company, called Wire and Plastic Products, named it WPP, and developed it into a vehicle for international acquisitions. A host of marketing companies were bought in a flurry. Nothing symbolized his determination more than his takeover of J. Walter Thompson. It was the first hostile takeover of an American advertising company to ever take place. Sorrell struck and succeeded and he went on to buy many other companies, including Ogilvy & Mather.

The international recession in the late 1980s damaged WPP. Although it had become the world's largest marketing services company, it was built upon a mountain of debt. The scale of the debt was too large to allow WPP's bankers to simply walk away from the company and let it collapse, but it proved to be a burden nevertheless, gravely undermining the value of the company, damaging WPP's growth momentum and business relationships, and hurting Sorrell's reputation.

Sorrell's confidence in his vision, above all else, held him and WPP afloat through the roughest seas. He understood the dynamics of the global economy, and he recognized that multinational business was set to accelerate in the coming years. He knew that companies like Pepsi-Cola, Ford, and Johnson & Johnson would expand their enterprises into more and more countries. At the same time, more and more people around the globe would be watching the same TV programs, sharing common fashions, and identifying themselves as part of the international community. A global perspective on marketing, Sorrell understood, would exploit the growing sense of international community and more efficiently serve genuinely global corporations.

Sorrell was right. Increasing numbers of companies want comprehensive, integrated ranges of services. The existence of a global provider of such services is a response to mounting demands that is certain to pay off. Sorrell is correct in his recognition that marketing will be one of the dynamic growth industries of the coming decades. In 1993, worldwide marketing expenditures by all firms amounted to $755 billion. That number is likely to double in the next few years.

Sorrell provided a detailed articulation of his vision and what it means for WPP's work in the company's 1993 annual report. He bluntly described the goal "to be the leading multi-national marketing services company" and stressed that this implied the need "to understand and satisfy the increasingly complex marketing needs of our clients at every level from the local to worldwide."

The vision stressed the critical requirement of customer satisfaction, but also the importance of securing staff loyalty and confidence. The statement noted WPP goals:

> To provide clients with a comprehensive and, when appropriate, integrated range of marketing services of the highest quality, both strategically and tactically ... to grow and maintain companies of such excellence that they provide the most stimulating career opportunities for talented professionals in all disciplines ... to provide those professionals with rewards and incentives which encourage the greatest number to a sense of ownership.[2]

Benetton

Another example of a brilliant vision turned into a successful reality is Benetton. Through the power of an idea, supported by excellent management, it has become one of the world's best known clothing brands. Benneton boasts of 7,000 stores in 110 countries and sales of over $1.6 billion—and it is barely 20 years old. Luciano Benetton, along with his sister and two brothers, saw a world emerging in which distinctive, many-colored fashions would appeal to a youthful generation in scores of countries.

Benneton, explaining one of the most important elements in his company's success, stated:

> The ability to have an open mind, be open to working with others, open to the stimuli that comes from abroad, from sectors other than our own, from different cultures, from anywhere in the world, is essential ... whenever new opportunities arise, we want to be ready to take advantage of them, regardless of where they are located geographically.[3]

This is easy to state, but difficult to practice. Benetton's novel approach can serve as a model for others. The company's founders, determined to maintain their vision, recognize that they must be acutely sensitive to changing trends and ideas among the world's youth. Their means of keeping current is through the new "Fabrica, United Colors and Form Research Center," which is inviting approximately 30 young people over the age of 18 (at Benetton's expense) for periods of between three and twelve months to work together to create new ideas. Says Luciano Benetton:

> The scholarship recipients will be selected from all over the world, based on their merits in the applied arts: design, graphics, photography, video, workmanship in textiles, wood, metals, and ceramics. The goal is to establish and develop a link between various cultures and traditions, and, in so doing, to reconcile individual needs for expression with the requirement of industrial communication and development.

Arrogance

In this chapter, we have stressed the winning approaches of entrepreneurs willing to pursue clear visions of building global businesses. There is a danger, however, that early successes can lead to arrogance, with the successful entrepreneur believing that he cannot do wrong and that his vision is so perfect that success is inevitable.

Going global is a complex business, and it demands the constant reexamination of the validity of a business vision. So swiftly are world business conditions changing now—and the tempo will accelerate as the new Industrial Revolution grows—that what may be a brilliant view one year could be inappropriate a year later. The examples that follow should serve as warnings of the dangers of arrogance in the global business environment.

Robert Maxwell and Globalization

The trouble may start, for example, when an entrepreneur believes he can, without additional support, think globally and act locally at the same time. Over-reaching can spell disaster. Few international empires have grown as rapidly as Robert Maxwell's. Maxwell was driven by a vision of building the world's largest publishing conglomerate, which would not only yield vast profits, but provide its owner with grand political power. Within a dozen years from the mid-1970s, Maxwell built an empire embracing publishing enterprises across the globe, from Jerusalem to New York, from Kenya to the United Kingdom. He died under mysterious circumstances, and, soon thereafter, the U.K. authorities discovered that he had presided over a massively bankrupt conglomerate. His is an example of almost unprecedented multinational corporate failure.

As his empire expanded throughout the 1970s and the 1980s, Maxwell convinced himself there was no company too big for him to swallow. Instead of consolidating his business, he leveraged his assets by accumulating ever more debt, and then he bought ever more companies, leveraged the new assets, and bought still more companies. The more enterprises he acquired to implement his vision, the more remote he became from managing the detailed business plans of his new acquisitions, and, inevitably, the quality of overall control of the empire eroded.

Maxwell could see the President in the White House, the bosses in the Kremlin, and the Prime Minister in London, tell them what he thought, and have pictures of himself with these leaders reproduced in newspapers around the globe. He spoke 10 languages, and he was as at home with the customs of Budapest as he was with the style of Paris. He believed he knew more about the world of business and its prospects than anyone else. He was consumed with his vision, underestimating both the rising levels of competition in the markets that he had entered and the mounting complexity of managing a business engaged in many publishing sectors in an increasing number of countries.

Increasingly, the Maxwell vision lost touch with the realities of the business world and the complexities of global management. He became overextended, and his empire started to collapse. His story is a warning that the more far-flung the business becomes and the more multinational it is, the more complicated the roles of corporate leaders become.

Wriston and Citibank

There was a lot of merit in the Maxwell vision, given that new technologies were making it more possible than ever to link diverse publishing businesses on a global scale, but, as the Maxwell story illustrates, early success can produce arrogance and overconfidence. Walter Wriston, who led Citibank in New York in the 1970s and early 1980s, also had a global vision, and he too was to become a victim of overconfidence. Wriston failed to appreciate that his vision of being the global banker to the world's sovereign governments was poorly timed. Like many other bankers, Wriston recognized in the 1970s that new and vast markets were opening in the Third World and that massive deposits could be won from the oil sheikhs of the Middle East.

Wriston's determination to make his institution into the largest global bank resulted in his executives being extremely aggressive in forging new business relationships around the world. The sheikhs placed ever more money in the hands of Citibank and other major banks, and the pressure increased down the ranks to make loans. Billions of dollars passed from the banks to Third World governments, and the Wriston vision moved rapidly towards a full reality.

The momentum accelerated as Wriston and his troops toured the globe, always willing to provide new loans to foreign governments. Wriston reasoned that governments never went broke. As the bank's lending volume grew, Wriston failed to challenge his assumptions and look at the hard facts, facts that showed that many countries were building vast mountains of debt.

Wriston and his senior subordinates stayed in almost identical Hilton-type hotels in Buenos Aires, Mexico City, Caracas, and Sao Paulo and confined their meetings with worldly officials and businessmen to posh restaurants. They were praised around the world, and Wriston was widely quoted in the leading newspapers as one of the most forthright and brilliant of international bankers.

However, Wriston failed to look closely at the cold facts on debt and to meet with enough opposition leaders and other critics in the Third World. He was surprised when, in mid-1982, the Mexican government announced that it could not service its foreign debts. Soon thereafter, a score of leading Third World countries, each of which owed billions of dollars to Citibank, also announced that they lacked the cash to pay their foreign bills and repay their loans.

It took more than a decade for Citibank to fully recover from its mistakes. It took a brilliant executive, William Rhodes, working with Wriston's successor, John Reed, years of agonizing, nonstop negotiations to lead Citibank and many of America's largest banks out of the Latin debt mess. Wriston's basic vision of seeing Third World growth as offering a huge banking opportunity was valid, but his overconfidence resulted in the failure to constantly reexamine assumptions, restructure strategies in the light of new developments, and ensure that all the necessary managerial safeguards were in place.

Translating a Vision into Goals

A vision is usually very broad and very general. Therefore, its translation into an active "business plan" demands setting goals. It is fascinating to read some of the annual reports of major enterprises and note that only a handful present to their shareholders both their vision of the company's place in a rapidly evolving world economy and the specific goals that the corporation's management is striving to achieve within that vision.

> "Transforming a vision into an active business plan requires setting real and achievable goals."

A company's vision is its leading edge—it represents what the company will be. Businessmen like Nelson, Sorrell, and Benetton are at the forefront because they have more clearly understood how the world's markets are evolving than have many of their rivals. They have been ahead of the game, and they continue to show equal skill in redefining their corporations for the new era. Their corporations have demonstrated an ability to adapt to new global conditions and to review the basic vision in the light of new developments in their markets. These corporations have built excellent management teams that are able to put hard analysis at the fore, rather than be overcome by arrogance.

The successes of WPP, Reuters, and Benetton set examples for others and underscore yet another aspect of the incredible range of changes in business and international relations that lie ahead, changes all prompted by the emergence of sophisticated, rapidly growing economies in the Third World.

15

Redefining the Corporation — Setting Goals

The largest multinational enterprises are now driving hard into every corner of the globe in search of new markets, simultaneously forced and aided by the increasing competitive pressures and new techniques of the economic boom. To succeed in this intensely competitive environment, corporations must redefine their basic approaches to doing business, and investors need to steer clear of those corporations that fail to do so. Entrepreneurs, managers, and investors must plan for an era of growth where the balance of profit centers shifts from the traditional markets to the newer, emerging ones; where the face of the corporate labor force becomes much more multicultural; and where national borders become less significant in charting corporate strategies.

> "National borders will become less significant in charting corporate changes."

Some corporations have concluded that the new challenges and opportunities demand whole new strategic approaches. Toys 'R' Us, for example, has been a very successful American company, but it recognized the limits of concentrating on the U.S. market alone. Toys 'R' Us has redefined its corporate strategy and is now expanding its business into foreign markets. "As we go forward, we see a much larger percentage of our growth being generated from foreign countries. In time there is no reason why we shouldn't be everywhere in the world," said Chairman Charles Lazarus in a 1973 interview with *Barron's* magazine.[1]

In late 1993, only 20 percent of the company's total sales of $1.4 billion were made outside the U.S., but Lazarus's vision sees international business generating 50 percent of its total revenues by 1997–98. This kind of expansion cannot be accomplished without a great deal of thought and study. "There are differences between markets," Lazarus said. "But," he continued, "there is a lot (that is) the same."

Integrating the differences and maximizing the potential of the similarities is part of the evolution that Toys 'R' Us and scores of other companies are confronting. The redefinition process is fundamental even to Japan's largest enterprises, which have long prided themselves on aggressively maximizing international opportunities. In mid-1994, two of the largest Japanese companies, Toshiba and Hitachi, separately took full-page advertisements in the *Financial Times* to highlight their struggles to become global.

President Tsutomu Kanai of Hitachi noted that the rise of the yen has, over the years, forced Japanese companies to strengthen their overseas investments. Boosting export prices is a limited and sometimes difficult option. He says:

> We are attempting to make the strong currency work to our advantage by sourcing more components outside of Japan and by raising the portion of overseas production in our total sales . . . about one-third of our overseas business is overseas production. This represents a major shift in focus over the last decade. Raising the level of off-shore production has two sides. We must also consider the position of our employees and plants in Japan. It is important that we restructure our domestic operations—for example, to shift production to more higher, value-added, and technically sophisticated products—in tandem with raising off-shore output. Restructuring in

this manner cannot be achieved quickly, but we are determined to realize our goal as soon as possible.[2]

Part of Hitachi's strategy is to develop a range of partnerships around the globe with IBM of the U.S., Olivetti of Italy, Goldstar Electron of Korea, and a growing list of others. If this strategy works, asserts Kanai, "The number of different markets in which we are seen to do business as insiders will grow larger and larger. This will make us truly a global corporation, and this is what I am looking forward to."

At Toshiba, President and CEO Fumio Sato talks about new global strategies from foundations of massive international sales generated from exports, 30 foreign production locations, and more than 80 foreign business bases. Sato declares:

> We do not think this kind of approach to globalization is sufficient, nor do we believe it can continue in its present form. It doesn't help us to deal with lower levels of competitiveness triggered by the yen's appreciation or the stronger competition we meet from products in our domestic market. We see our operations as forming more of a network linking equals, with Tokyo as an important center, but not the only one. We expect an erosion of the borders between Japan and overseas and see truly global operations as borderless.[3]

Sato notes that:

> Transcending borders in its global organization will give Toshiba greater flexibility in all aspects of our operations. We will be able to respond more promptly to political and economic changes and deal more effectively with such problems as currency appreciation and trade imbalances.

Commenting on a familiar theme, Sato says,

> In the global network we are aiming for, business must develop along both global and local lines. Some products are becoming increasingly international in nature. Products like electronic components, which are built to international standards, with only very limited local variation, should be manufactured for the world market at whichever places best ensure our international competitiveness.

> But then there are products that meet specific local needs and demands. Household appliances are designed for very localized needs and markets and need to be developed, manufactured, and sold within that

market. Toshiba embarked on production of commercial-use air conditioners in the U.K. in 1991, in addition to color television sets, in order to provide products suiting the European lifestyle. This selection of production sites, which best match the character of the product, along with diversification of procurement (using many different international sources), is the foundation for a global logistics network.

Many companies in developing countries that grew strong as low-cost producers of manufactured goods for foreign markets and as basic suppliers to rapidly rising domestic markets are now transforming themselves into global enterprises. They see the new Industrial Revolution coming and are in its vanguard. For them, the need to be universal is compelling.

In the redefinition, therefore, Daewoo Group of Korea, for example, is no longer focused on the world's most advanced countries for its major future growth. In 1994 alone, according to a *Wall Street Journal* report, the company planned to commit some $8 billion to make and sell its products in Eastern Europe, Central Asia, and Latin America. It is an example of a trend that will increasingly be seen: the most successful Third World companies seeking expansion outside of their countries in the rapidly evolving, poorer parts of the Third World.

Articulating a Vision

As they redefine their businesses and seek to implement far-reaching visions, corporations are setting broad goals for new strategic plans. However, a goal is meaningless unless set within a distinct timeframe with distinct and achievable deadlines. Every member of the team must know the goals and be committed to their attainment. Time has to be spent on defining goals, testing them, and articulating them well.

Articulating the vision and specifying the goals in a global context is increasingly the core challenge of executive leadership today. Tomorrow, increasing numbers of shareholders will be demanding that corporate leaders spell out their detailed goals on a full, international basis. Shareholders might argue that the world has become too complex and fast-moving for an ordinary investor to keep up with the changes. Accordingly, the shareholder might reason, it is all the more important for corporate leaders to define clear goals to maintain the confidence of their shareholders. This means articulating goals for different markets and sectors in ways that all shareholders and all other stakeholders in the corporation—employees, suppliers, customers, and sources of finance—can understand.

In the largest corporations, it is fashionable to stress decentralization in global management and to spread responsibility as widely as possible. The danger of this approach is that goals can become solely financial or products-oriented. This narrow concept of goals can fail to take into account the shifting sands of economic integration and the increasing relationships between the new markets.

3M, Minnesota Mining and Manufacturing, monitored developments in Europe and concluded that the rapid integration of the 15 countries of the European Union demanded a major overhaul of 3M's approaches. Its goals were clear: to ensure that it could maximize the opportunities being created by the rapid reduction of borders between European countries; the harmonization of business rules and regulations between European countries; and the prospect of the establishment of a common European market for an expanding number of Western and Eastern European countries. 3M's organization had been largely based on single, national markets in Europe.

3M's new approach was illustrated in an article in the *Financial Times* in November 1993, highlighting Claire-Noelle Bigay, 29, a marketing professional at 3M who had worked solely in France until the reorganization. Now, Ms. Bigay is a member of a six-person core team of marketing experts for a 3M line of products, with responsibilities spanning all of the European Union countries. Her immediate colleagues are two Britons in the U.K., a Dutch woman in Germany, and a Belgian and an Italian, both based in Belgium. Although Ms. Bigay still spends a lot of time in France seeing local customers, she has broadened her direct product base into Germany as well (she speaks German as fluently as she does English), while also being a coordinator for distinct product lines through the Euro-wide core team. As the *Financial Times* summed-up:

> Bigay is one of about 1,000 managers at almost every level within 3M in Europe, many of them in their 20s and 30s, whose lives have been transformed this year. As part of a radical reshaping of the company's European organization, they have been given significant product responsibilities across national borders. [4]

To meet its European goals, 3M thoroughly reorganized, and today, in fact, it has 15 "European Business Centers" for its range of products and services. Goals are a means of keeping track of progress, especially in an environment of ever-growing and complicated pressures from investors who are thinking and acting globally, governmental regulators who are trying to set global standards, non-governmental watchdog organizations who are monitoring the activities of the major multinational firms on a global basis, and international organizations who are worrying about the rising trade power of major corporations (more than 50 percent of all world trade is intrafirm, that is, exporting and importing from one country to another within a single corporation). All of these realities need to be reflected in a company's goals.

As corporations define goals, set targets, and implement plans, the availability of first-class information is essential. The world has become far too complicated for business people to succeed on the basis of intuition and gut feelings alone. The striking charactistic of the leaderships of companies like Daimler-Benz, Ford, Royal Dutch Shell, Coca-Cola, and many others is the degree to which they invest in obtaining excellent basic information and the efficiency with which they translate this information into the decision-making process. Managers must have a knowledge of markets and of what competitors are doing. They must also have the knowledge to know how best to acquire excellent information. We will discuss the importance of obtaining knowledge in Chapter 17.

> **"To secure the best information, top management must develop external contacts of the highest quality."**

At the same time, to secure the best information and to ensure the most efficient approaches to strategic implementation and the swiftest path to maximum new market positioning, top management must develop external contacts of the highest quality (see Chapter 18). This is one of the greatest challenges in international business today. Microsoft determined that to obtain the best information and contacts in China, it needed Chinese partners. The company is willing to share its profits and prospects with these partners, recognizing this is the price it must pay for the best contacts.

All business is based on relationships, and building relationships in scores of countries simultaneously is as much a science today as it is an art. It is a skill that more and more companies are learning, and, as they do, their international influence will mount. The types of contacts being sought must range from government and international development agencies to potential joint venture partners, new suppliers, and new customers.

Positioning for Advantage

Corporations entering markets for the first time need to ensure that they get the quickest and most efficient new business start. This effort demands developing a strong presence, a clear image within target markets, and keen awareness of the urgency in new markets to establish reputations of the highest integrity (see Chapter 19). Coca-Cola does this brilliantly by investing heavily in every new market it enters and then sustaining high visibility in a highly skilled fashion. Many other firms stumble in this effort.

Some enter Third World countries with all too evident airs of arrogance and superiority. As a result, they encounter rude awakenings in confrontations with ministers, officials, and local business rivals with worldly knowledge, excellent education, and considerable self-confidence. No longer can a U.S. executive with little international experience expect that his or her company's name will make all local people shudder, bow, and scrape. The world is very different today and will be even more different tomorrow.

16

Redefining the Corporation — Cultural Changes

R
edefining the corporation for the boom ahead requires nothing less than a total reappraisal of a corporation's culture. Few corporations are doing this fast enough.

As companies become more multinational, they may well confront basic conflicts between an old, entrenched culture and the need to build a new one that is far more able to make money across the globe. The fact is, the more global a company becomes, the more diversity it has among its employees in terms of ethnicity, nationality, language, and tradition. Building such a diverse labor force into an effective team is one of the toughest management challenges of modern times.

The circumstances at two very different, but equally global organizations—the World Bank and American Express—illustrate just how tough this challenge is. The World Bank, now 50 years old, has been the leading development assistance agency and has brought together several thousand of the world's best economists from 100 different countries. Although it has done outstanding work, the World Bank is widely

> "Redefining the corporation for the boom ahead requires nothing less than a total reappraisal of a corporation's culture."

seen as bloated and bureaucratic. Part of the explanation is that, in spite of all its international experience, it has had difficulty creating a culture common to all of the diverse nationalities on its staff. As a result, the World Bank uses impossibly long reports and endless committee meetings as the central forms of resolving issues, because these are the least intimidating approaches to decision making when so many nationals are involved. Needless to say, this can be an inefficient process; however, changing the culture has proven to be a nightmare for several outstanding managers.

A. W. Clausen, who saved and rebuilt the Bank of America in the mid-1980s, failed to win full control of the World Bank's multi-cultured bureaucracy and trim the administrative budget in meaningful fashion when he served as its president from 1981 to 1986. Clausen greatly strengthened the Bank's work in Africa and ensured that the Bank was aggressive in assisting countries to adopt free market policies, but the external image of an inefficient institution grew during his tenure. The late Lewis Preston, who had brilliantly guided J. P. Morgan through very tough times, was no more successful in changing this image than Clausen when running the World Bank from 1991 to early 1995. He ensured that the Bank became a major influence in Central and Eastern Europe, and he forged new links for it with private business, but he could not change the perception that the Bank was overly bureaucratic.

The new president of the World Bank, investment banker James Wolfensohn, who took office in June 1995, will have no alternative but to devote a great deal of time to the challenge of finding ways to make people from scores of nationalities and diverse cultures blend together in highly cost-efficient teams that can be effective partners for multinational investors and for emerging economies. He is likely to push for a major decentralization of the World Bank, placing far more responsibility in field offices and thinning managerial ranks. He will strive to make this public sector institution run more like a business, promoting concepts of risk taking over consensus building. The challenge before him is difficult, and he might be tempted to bring to the World Bank some of the best experiences to be found in the business world.

American Express is an example of a company that has repeatedly redefined itself as its global market has changed. It has also successfully confronted the issue of corporate culture in an enterprise serving and employing people in more than 160 countries. Indeed, it is as well known in remote parts of China as it is in New York. It has a brand name that has been cultivated with enormous success by adapting its services and its approaches to local markets, while at the same time maintaining a genuinely universal brand image. It has long understood that it had to define, and then anchor, a distinct brand image that would make people in scores of nations as proud to work for the company as to buy its products. That is why today you find the same card, the same slogans, the same color schemes on American Express advertising, labels, and note paper across the globe. To achieve this success, American Express tailored its actual operating strategies to diverse local market conditions. In every instance the company has focused on the brand and the attributes that customers associate with it—security, integrity, commitment, customer service, global presence, and recognition. It has drummed into all of its staff a set of corporate values that are universal and that are at the leading edge of its whole marketing approach.

In recent years, the leadership of American Express took success for granted and sought, despite inexperience and an increasingly competitive credit card market, to move beyond its marketing base. The company diversified, overspent, and got into trouble, and, in early 1993, chairman James Robinson was forced out. Soon thereafter, American Express sold most of its investment banking/brokerage subsidiaries and readied itself to return to its core activities and concentrate on international marketing.

American Express's Travel-Related Services subsidiary, the lead entity within the Amex group and a prime source of its global marketing success, is an area run by Harvey Golub, who became CEO in February 1993 and chairman in August of that year. Over the years, this group developed new product and service launches into a fine, highly detailed, and very expensive art form. Under Golub's overall direction, it began acquiring other corporations in the travel-related fields, building new energy and vitality for itself in the process (one of its major acquisitions was the U.S. and international corporate travel management businesses of rival Thomas Cook). The company is aiming to be faster to market with new product and service offerings.

An important aspect of American Express's approach was concern by top management not to go too far in defining every minute detail of a global strategy implementation. The goals were clear, but there was intense sensitivity to consulting with individual American Express managers, country-by-country, to define local market strategies. This meticulous setting of goals and determination to distinguish between global goals and local strategies has set American Express apart and made it a success. Its achievement underscores the need for multinationals to constantly examine their basic corporate goals and repeatedly ensure that corporate strategies are accurately reflecting these goals.[1]

Thinking globally, acting locally: This is one of the keys to genuine multinational corporate success. Every market is different. You may have universal goals, but the strategies needed to reach those goals have to be precisely tailored to the individual markets in which you seek to develop business. One of the best methods for understanding local markets is to involve local managers.

> "One of the best methods for understanding local markets is to involve local managers."

Multicultural Management

The composition of personnel in an enterprise needs to change rapidly as the company expands internationally. One of the most fascinating aspects of the new world of business is the incredible national and ethnic diversity among the ranks of the employees of single corporations. Nestlé of Switzerland has hundreds of plants across the world, employing people of every nationality. Indeed, only 7,000 of its 218,000 employees work in the country of Switzerland, its headquarters.

As corporations like Nestlé, Ford, J. P. Morgan, Pepsi-Cola, and an increasing number of others are showing, the more multinational a business becomes, the more it must seek to recruit outstanding international individuals into its top ranks. Without this mix, the corporate culture will remain too traditional. Some of the leaders of the world's largest and most multinational corporations are reviewing their approaches and questioning whether their personnel policies are adequate for the new challenges ahead. Interestingly, this is happening as much in Japan as in Europe, even though just a few years ago it would have been almost unthinkable to imagine non-Japanese holding top executive posts in the largest Japanese enterprises. Recently, however, the unthinkable has become the thinkable for those who most clearly see the full impact and opportunity of the aproaching boom.

> "The more multinational a business becomes, the more it must seek to recruit outstanding foreign individuals into its top ranks."

Mitsubishi Corporation's President and CEO, Minaru Makihara, is at the forefront in planning for corporate cultural change. He is concerned with transforming a corporation that has traditionally scanned the globe through a distinctly Japanese perspective into an enterprise where no nationality is dominant and where Japan is only one among its many national sites of importance. The Mitsubishi chief, who studied at Harvard University and who has spent more than two decades working outside of Japan, has the knowledge and practical experience of the world to open his company to the fullest extent to non-Japanese and foreign cultures, thereby becoming genuinely global.

Mitsubishi Corporation has more than 180 offices and branches and almost 600 subsidiaries around the world. In a 1994 interview, Makihara noted:

> There is a need for us to move beyond our traditional Japan-oriented business and develop stronger corporate relationships with firms around the world. With the advent of the global economy, and to ensure stable growth in the future, we must continuously seek out new markets and find new ways to meet the business needs of our partners worldwide ... In this process, it has become necessary for us to reexamine our current personnel structure. Due to the historically Japan-oriented

nature of our business, the bulk of our overseas management positions have tended to be filled by Japanese nationals on temporary assignment. To keep up with the changing circumstances, it is imperative that we further open such positions to our non-Japanese staff.[2]

Evidently, Makihara accepts the view of the late Akio Morita, founder of Sony and the most international of Japanese executives, who believed that "global localization" is the concept that enables companies to take fullest advantage of global economies of scale and yet be fast on their feet in rapidly changing local market situations. Makihara explains:

> As we become more international, there is a simultaneous need for us to become more truly localized. Practically speaking, our ability to respond to our customers in each country or region will be bolstered to the extent that our staff on location is intimately familiar with the customs, language, and norms of the local market. Logically, those best suited to the task are those with extensive, long-term experience in the area.

For Mitsubishi to become what its chief executive calls a "sound global enterprise," it must, he noted:

> Maintain a unified corporate identity. We must work harder to train, develop, and promote our locally-hired staff. Language is certainly an issue, but a firm understanding of the corporate history, mission, and practices cannot be underestimated. We are now working to create the most appropriate personnel system to complement our efforts to grow beyond our traditional Japanese business.

Global Administration

The process of change and development essential for being competitive in international business demands that managers juggle a large number of balls at one time. As they seek to redefine the corporate culture, they must, at the same time, convert largely single-nation-oriented administrative systems into fully fledged multinational ones. This raises fundamental issues of corporate control and the roles of corporate leadership, budget management, personnel, and training. Running and supervising operations that are thousands of miles distant from the head office poses control challenges for managers, who have little experience with such situations.

To that end, however, there is a growing number of experts today who can assist in these tasks—structuring international pay scales and benefit packages, opening global banking relationships, overseeing international real estate rentals and acquisitions, and hosts of other important matters.

One such matter is the establishment of international communications systems. As the Internet, e-mail, fax, and telephone come on stream in even the most remote corners of the emerging countries, there is an increasing sense that interactive communications across the world will shrink the planet still more, accelerate the pace of transactions and information sharing, and add whole new dimensions to global business and business administration.

Ways of thinking and, hence, managing corporate administration are going to be increasingly challenged as globalization takes hold. For example, many service companies have traditionally developed national and regional administrative systems in which a successful executive in London might advance up a European organizational line of command and be considered for responsibilities beyond Europe when he or she had reached senior European levels. As technology binds markets across the globe, maintaining such a system may be redundant because clients of service companies think globally, not regionally.

For example, at WPP the national and regional organizational structure has been abandoned to enable the company to better meet client demands. Promotions are now made on a client basis, with the executive being given responsibility for a client on a worldwide basis. Moreover, increasing resources are being invested in worldwide client responsibilities, and marketing services companies' income statements are now being split on a client, functional, and geographic basis rather than on a purely national or regional basis.

As WPP points out in its 1993 annual report, this change creates

> ...a number of organizational problems for marketing service companies, just as it has done for clients. Agency personnel will have to become used to having three bosses instead of one. They will have to think three-dimensionally—by client, by function, and by geography. Geographic fiefdoms and baronies will be less effective, and cooperative structures more important. This mirrors the changes taking place by clients, and the reduction in power of the country manager. Recent client reorganizations on a worldwide scale, as well as regional coordinations, will accelerate these trends.

Inevitably, as companies restructure and reorganize to meet new global demands, increasing numbers of individuals in a single firm become involved in activities in more countries, touch upon corporate/governmental relationships in these countries, and possibly, influence the corporation's global image in these countries. Managing these activities and relationships is a formidable, yet essential, administrative challenge.

The key consideration is ensuring that those new hires are loyal to the corporation; full commitment to corporate goals is imperative. To achieve this loyalty, corporations must be willing to offer meaningful, long-term incentives—usually cash and career opportunities. Success is also predicated on the placement of local nationals—that is, nationals from the countries in which the multinational corporations do business—into managerial positions of mounting importance. It is often difficult at first to find the right people, and training is critical, but there is no better means of building a strong sense of a single, global, corporate culture among employees than by demonstrating through promotions that there are no nationality barriers to entry to the highest levels of the company. For example, the current president of Chrysler is a Swiss who worked for Ford and BMW in Germany before moving to the United States. Or, to take another example, McKinsey & Co. selected an Indian, Rajat Gupta, as its Managing Director in 1994. Born in India, educated in the United States, and having worked extensively in Europe, Gupta had the perfect profile to meet the global approaches of this leading management consulting firm.[3]

Hiring globally is a crucial component for companies concerned with evolving effective internal communications in an enterprise undergoing the fundamental shift from a domestic to a global character. It is this consideration that prompts, for example, Coca-Cola Chairman and CEO Robert C. Goizueta to use every opportunity to stress that his firm is "effectively led by our multi-cultural, multi-national, senior management team."[4]

Training for Global Business

The more multinational the company, its staff, and all its diverse components, the more important training becomes. Multinational managers must meet regularly and learn constantly about the company and its management approaches, as well as the new techniques that are being applied across the board. The investment in staff training to build a common, vibrant, global corporate culture is likely to be substantial, and too often companies devote minimal resources to this activity because they find it hard to translate training explicitly into bottom line value. However, training of management staff is fundamental to building a cohesive multinational corporation with an effective culture. Without it, the results can be disastrous.

> "The more multinational the company, its staff, and all its diverse components, the more important training becomes."

Today, Citibank strives to hire as many foreign nationals as possible and use local people as much as it can in its growing global empire, yet it has centralized all of its key staff training programs to ensure the development of a common corporate culture across the world—a culture that can readily buy into the central vision of the bank's top executives, translate broad corporate goals into local market goals, acquire the knowledge and contacts that benefit the multinational enterprise as a whole, and attack positioning in ways that are fully in keeping with the corporation's overall standards and values.

Internal Corporate Relations

As the corporation becomes more international, relationships between divisions within the single firm can become more difficult to manage. Bringing diverse divisions into a common culture and into partnerships and team relationships with one another is a delicate and difficult task that can be subject to intense strains. Corporate leaders must ensure that domestic divisions do not feel demoted or of secondary importance as the company moves into the international arena. At the same time, fledgling international divisions dare not start life with inferiority complexes relative to the traditional, larger, domestic divisions. Only top management can deal with this issue. Often management is too busy to confront it until bitter rivalries have already emerged between the domestic and the international divisions. The schisms can become gravest when overall corporate profits are weak, and top management seeks to implement cost-cutting programs. Building the right relationships represents an important challenge to management skills.

For corporate leadership, a key issue is ensuring that the overall process of going global is well-coordinated in terms of the corporate culture. The corporate communications department can assume a central role in this regard. As the company changes, it is essential that top management fully understand the scale of corporate cultural transformation and see the bottom line benefits of evolving a unified sense of corporate values and goals among all employees, regardless of where they are located.

The style of internal communications is integral to establishing a new cultural awareness within a domestic corporation that goes international and within a multinational enterprise that rapidly broadens its range of worldly activities. Ford, for example, has invested heavily to ensure that its corporate communications are effective at a time of major corporate cultural change. It has moved to common governance of product, manufacturing, supply, and sales activities along global product lines, which demands sophisticated corporate communications to all employees in all countries. Ford has a daily television program that reaches almost all employees around the world through a satellite television system.

The modes of communicating within the multinational firm must be adapted to the differing cultures and values in each of the foreign markets the company enters. This is an area requiring sensitivity and skill, because a corporation's external image is frequently determined by the views and attitudes of its own employees. Too often, internal and external communications are treated distinctly. Securing and ensuring coordination between them is a difficult test for the leadership of the corporate communications function in the multinational enterprise.

An all too common error is leaving overall strategies to headquarters and then hiring an array of local advertising agencies to implement all foreign external relations. Finding the optimum balance is difficult, and most American corporations have not yet found it. They tend to give international corporate communications (internal and external) merely token acknowledgement, leaving such matters almost entirely to the managements of foreign subsidiaries and affiliates, who in turn, assign these responsibilities to local firms— frequently advertising agencies. While it is tempting to farm-out all manner of public relations and advertising functions through foreign subsidiaries, this results in a significant lack of central knowledge and control.

Very few top corporate communications executives at the largest U.S. multinational enterprises are able to demonstrate knowledge and experience with regard to global issues such as employee communications, investor relations, governmental affairs, media relations, and strategies for other key external constituencies. This kind of expertise is going to be in increasing demand at fast-moving multinational corporations.

Face-to-face discussions between the chiefs of corporate communications and top corporate managers in affiliates abroad about building such expertise around these issues are rare. Indeed, many heads of corporate communications in multinational companies rarely travel abroad for the express purpose of strengthening their networks with field executives and ensuring the comprehensive coordination of corporation-wide external and internal communications. Too often, in other words, U.S. corporate communications become stuck in the traditional, domestic U.S. mindset, while the corporation as a whole is moving rapidly into a genuinely global era. The same applies to Japanese and European companies.

As a corporation enters new markets and takes on new foreign staff, it must ensure that these new employees understand the corporate culture, its approaches, its values, and the importance it attaches to excellent staff relations. Far too few corporations in the multinational arena have senior executives in their central corporate communications departments who have any understanding of the complexity and the importance of communicating to employees in a diverse, multinational arena.

Carole M. Howard, who for many years held the post of Vice-President and Director of Public Relations and Communications Policy, Reader's Digest Association, Inc., believes that

If your company is going global, you should be at the forefront of its effort to position itself in the worldwide marketplace. Organizations with a global business strategy also need a global communications strategy—with agreement on objectives, priority messages, target publics, and product promotion plans from New York to New Zealand, so each country's public relations activities not only support local operations but also reinforce the corporation's global plan ... our antennae must be up wherever our organizations do business all over the globe.

Doing this well results in synergies among all the component parts of the global empire. Doing it well means that staff across the globe are thinking about the same corporate cultural identity and working in ways that seem in absolute harmony. Howard states that:

All our international companies prepare a public relations plan as part of their annual business plans. The public relations plans are based on local issues, local markets, and local products—but they all bear a remarkable similarity to each other because they also are based on the company's global communications strategy.[5]

The corporate redefinition process is continual. Some leading multinationals have taken giant strides to redefine themselves along the lines noted earlier in this chapter and to position their administrations for vast new global challenges. In coming years, the new competitive pressures from the emerging economies will force most multinational enterprises to rethink their visions, their goals, and their approaches to defining corporate culture. It will be a new and dramatic phase in the annals of corporate reengineering—this time, on a fully global basis.

17

Global Knowledge Acquistion and Training

Rupert Murdoch has the determination of a ruthless entrepreneur and the ability to create a vision for his enterprises of global scale. He also has an additional attribute, without which he would be a failure: an unquenchable appetite for knowledge. The pace of global business developments is so dramatic today that knowledge about every aspect of world economic change has to be central to a winning globalization strategy. In recent years, Murdoch, the head of News Corporation, has taken giant steps towards building a global empire. Time and again he has beaten competitors because he has acquired the crucial market and political knowledge ahead of rivals.

> "Knowledge and contacts are the prime ingredients for turning entrepreneurial vision into relationships."

In a 1994 interview, Murdoch left no doubt about the basis of his global business vision: "The marriage of the satellite and the computer and the television camera is just changing the whole world. If you don't get with it in the media, you're going to be marginalized and left behind."[1]

To succeed, he has forged a critical alliance with MCI and built an empire that includes FOX TV in the U.S.[2], El Canal Fox in Latin America, the largest newspaper group in Britain, BSKYB satellite television in Europe, and Star TV, which spans Asia. Murdoch is also doing deals at the highest political levels in China and India. Murdoch has understood, perhaps more clearly than most business people, that building a business intelligence network of international dimensions is absolutely vital in the new economic era. His network consists essentially of constant efforts by himself and his small entourage of trusted lieutenants to know what is happening politically and economically in every industrial and emerging market in the world, where to get information, and how to forge crucial contacts around the globe. Knowledge and contacts are the prime ingredients necessary for building strategies that can turn entrepreneurial visions into realities.

The Dynamics of Change

Successful international expansion demands a thorough understanding of the dynamics of the global economy—understanding which countries and groups of countries will expand fastest and slowest in the decade ahead and understanding the impact of these dynamics on the economic outlook for the rest of the world. In this chapter, we will seek to highlight the diversity of knowledge to which global entrepreneurs, managers, and investors must be sensitive, the importance of understanding how to value business intelligence, and aspects of how to make the key country selection choices. With almost 200 sovereign countries in today's world, the selection of new business locations is more complex than ever, and obtaining expert knowledge is worth its weight in gold.

The dynamics of change in the global business arena are producing ever-greater contrasts. On the one hand, entrepreneurs have visions of where global business is going, are able to obtain and digest masses of information, and act with courage and determination. On the other hand, executives are mired in corporate tradition, insecure about the international arena, and uncertain about how to obtain the knowledge vital to making sensible global decisions.

Companies often fail in the international arena because of lack of global and regional knowledge. Indeed, in a 1992 survey conducted by Deloitte Touche Tohmatsu International, fully one-quarter of 400 companies surveyed in 20 industrial countries had ceased overseas operations in the previous five years for one or more of the following reasons: the hoped-for market did not materialize, they experienced operational failures, they had problems with business partners, there were political conflicts in the sought-after market, or they experienced difficulties in securing payments. Above all, however, the respondents said that their greatest problem in preparing their foreign ventures was obtaining information.[3]

Following Competitors

To succeed, corporations must obtain a whole variety of different kinds of knowledge. They must have knowledge of competitors' approaches to global markets, global developments in specific business sectors, geopolitical global and regional trends, and specific details of target countries. In each of these areas, the failure to do comprehensive homework can be costly. For example, watching competitors is vital, but following competitors can be dangerous. Consider the following.

An executive hears that a rival company is establishing new operations in a particular foreign country and decides his firm should open there as well. His judgement is based almost solely on the actions of his rivals and some superficial, product-related market research. By the time he invests there, however, the target investment country is overcrowded with foreign enterprises and is confronting political and economic problems. By becoming a sheep and following the herd instead of conducting his own in-depth research, he has led his company toward a crash.

The point is, competitive information has to be gathered before money is invested. Imaginative decisions on where to locate new ventures in the international arena and how to organize such ventures demand a whole array of different kinds of information; the best business results go to those willing to make the effort to look beyond the conventional wisdom within their business sectors and search for brand new approaches, new locations for new markets, and new opportunities.

Knowledge Scenarios

There are scores of different ways to obtain necessary information, but none of them are cheap. The investments made today by the largest corporations in acquiring knowledge and analyzing it are vast. The process is often highly sophisticated, with some corporations undertaking in-depth research into fundamental economic and social trends. For example, John Wybrew of Shell U.K. Limited, a subsidiary of Royal Dutch Shell, asserts that its research prompted the conclusion that "Transferable technology and foreign direct investment in the emerging industrializing economies are adding rapidly to the competitive pressures on the mature high-cost economies of the OECD (leading industrial) countries."

Wybrew added:

> Accordingly, their industries are being compelled to apply advancing technology ever more actively, reorganizing and reducing costly manpower to achieve greater productivity. The consequent improvements in technology and work practice are then transferred, with investment, to the new industries of the emerging non-OECD (Third World) countries. This, in turn, reinforces the progress of economic and political liberalization—and so on back around the cycle. [4]

Because there are so many factors that can frustrate the progress of this cycle, the largest companies are subjecting it to rigorous analysis, putting together volumes of information and building knowledge scenarios. Only large firms can afford this sort of scenario modelling, but time and again they seem inclined to share their findings and, thereby, influence whole trends and modes of thinking.

The acquisition of knowledge is only part of the game. Business people must also understand how to use the knowledge they have acquired. This demands that the people who make the final decisions on where to expand abroad are trained to use the information wisely and within realistic frames of reference.

Leadership Sensitivity to Knowledge

This training needs to start with the business's top leadership, including the Board of Directors. Too often, a major corporation plans a huge foreign investment by merely bringing in a high-profile consultant to spread geopolitical information and comfort. The Directors ask a few questions—usually superficial ones—and make their decision. The fact is, few members of boards of U.S. companies are sufficiently sensitive to international political and economic trends.

At one of the largest U.S. electric power utilities, for example, top management and the Board had no experience in what giant corporations in the same sector overseas were doing. When the CEO visited utility companies in France and Germany, he was stunned by how advanced they were in many areas. He was also surprised to learn the degree to which these foreign companies were rapidly building businesses to secure new international markets. The CEO and his colleagues should have known all about international developments to ensure their corporation was modern, sophisticated, and competitive.

Moreover, those bringing the recommendations to the top managers and boards are often poorly trained as well. Many corporate managers who now have international responsibilities have inadequate training in basic geopolitics and economics; they rose to their current positions on the basis of their domestic performance and their management and technical skills. To counter this, many corporations are spending time and money on management training in international affairs, but rarely is it sufficient. Frequently, these are brief (two- or three-day), intensive training programs on broad topics such as "Doing Business in East Europe" or "The New Business Climate in Asia." While the quality of speakers and discussions in such seminars can be excellent, these programs amount to only a minor appetizer where a full meal is in order.

Substantive training in global geopolitics is imperative for executives leading business in the era ahead. That training will show how to differentiate between countries. The choices are getting wider today, as scores of countries have developed, or are in the process of developing, comprehensive investment codes to provide assurances on such issues as nonexpropriation of foreign assets, repatriation of dividends, withholding and other taxes, freedom of foreign exchange movements, international arbitration processes in the event of disputes, and multiple investment incentives.

In addition, training has to focus on the regulatory regimes that are evolving around the globe. A special report on international investment by the World Bank's Foreign Investment Advisory Service (FIAS) in 1992, for example, noted that:

> To the governments of most developing countries (East Europe should also be included here), the case for screening seems so compelling that few governments are completely open to foreign investment;

most have some mechanism to admit foreign investors selectively or to exercise some choice in allocating incentives. Countries vary widely, however, in the stringency of their entry regulations.[5]

FIAS added:

Most have general laws or regulations that prohibit foreign investment in certain industries, such as the distributive trade, local transportation, and utilities. Others prohibit substantial foreign ownership of firms or industries that are critical to the nation's defense. Some countries have an active policy of screening each investment (although the applicable criteria governing the decisions that are made may not be at all transparent).

Being trained to understand the diverse approaches (and to know where to swiftly obtain expert information) is crucial for managers engaging in international direct investment. The training in the formal sides of rules and regulations needs to go hand-in-hand with training in cultural issues.

A major financial institution, for example, lost vast sums by failing to adequately appreciate seemingly small, yet significant, differences in attitudes towards loan repayments in different cultures around the world. It had failed to undertake the necessary geopolitical/cultural investigations to secure first-class knowledge. In this case, the company assumed that people in many foreign countries would view credit card repayments in very similar ways to Americans. This proved to be entirely wrong, especially in numerous countries that had never experienced credit cards before.

Finally, no business today is immune to environmental factors. Every country is developing its own environmental rules and regulations. It is important to understand the global trends in these areas and the specifics as they relate to your particular business. For example, in mid–1992, a European entrepreneur devised a plan for the development of a new business concerned with environmental technologies. The logic of the approaches suggested that money was to be made, and environmental benefits to be secured, by building pilot plants in Brazil using their new technologies.

Optimally, the business would have shipped industrial residues from Italy, where present regulations make handling very difficult, to Brazil, where they could be turned into energy. The Brazilians would have received payments for taking the residues and then made additional income by turning the residues into energy. Logic was one thing, reality another.

Upon investigation, it was evident that, even though there would be minimal environmental damage to Brazil and tremendous foreign exchange earnings, existing political conventions around the world made the shipment of residues from Italy to Brazil impossible. Obtaining this knowledge at an early stage in the planning process was critical in avoiding costly expenditures. Conditions in many other countries were analyzed against a wealth of information on international approaches and policies towards the environment in general and waste management in particular. Decisions on country selection evolved as the product of accumulating a wide array of vital knowledge. This was not easy, but it was essential.

By the time the analysis had been completed, the geographical focus had switched from Latin America to Eastern Europe. The stage was now set to look in depth at the regional factors in Eastern Europe that would lead to a specific country selection decision.

Country Selection

With the aim of making key country selection choices for new global business, executives need to not only obtain knowledge of international political, economic, and regulatory developments as they influence their industries, but they must also match their broad global knowledge with more detailed intelligence on the specific geographic regions of greatest interest to them. Within this context, the types of knowledge that need to be considered include: economic policies prevailing in the geographic region of interest, special trade arrangements between countries within the region, and existing and prospective trade and investment agreements between these countries and the leading industrial countries (for example, the prospects for extending NAFTA).

Today, official international organizations and think tanks are producing masses of region-specific information. It is easy to be overwhelmed. Hiring experts to extract the essential information and present it in precise fashion is a useful investment, but it is only useful if the in-house senior staff knows how to digest and challenge the information supplied by these outside expert

consultants. Corporate managers need to be acutely aware, in particular, of the special regulations, laws, and treaties that govern
their products in the geographic regions of greatest interest to
them. They also need to have knowledge of the official regional
bloc trading groups that have emerged and that, in some cases,
are becoming increasingly important.[6]

From the general must come the specific. Obtaining absolutely
reliable and precise country data before country selections are made
and cash is spent is
essential. Reference
books, government in-
formation officers, and
even official interna-
tional statistics may all
too often present an
overly optimistic pic-
ture of a country, while
minimizing the potential difficulties. To overcome this, every bit
of data needs to be checked with individuals who have hands-on
business experience and who are reliable. The depth of knowledge obtained on everything from tax matters to political and macro-
economic factors serves to build a comprehensive picture. As the
picture becomes clearer, confidence in the wisdom of the final decision grows or, conversely, the questions start to arise that force
rethinking. For prudent business leaders, knowledge is the basis
of confidence.

> "Obtaining absolutely reliable and
> precise country data is essential."

Until recently, the number of countries that were viewed as major
opportunities for investment by multinational corporations was
relatively small. This is changing profoundly, and, in coming years,
we will see the list grow longer and longer as the new Industrial
Revolution gets into full stride. Asian countries in particular may
become much more prominent. The geopolitical understanding of
this was underscored in late 1993, when President Clinton welcomed 13 leaders from Asia to the first-ever Asia–Pacific Economic
Cooperation Summit. The President sought to allay European concerns by stressing that "Europe remains at the core of our alliances."
Then President Clinton said, "But, as our concern shifts to economic

challenges that are genuinely global, we must look across the
Pacific as well as the Atlantic. We must engage the world's fastest
growing economies."

The key to attracting foreign investment for emerging economies
rests in building an inviting business climate. As increasing numbers of governments recognize how important it is to establish a
meaningful, enabling environment—good economic policies, an open
and stable political climate, laws and regulations that are support-
ive of business and of foreign investment—and seek to implement
policies to create this environment, their countries will emerge as
sound locations for investment by multinational enterprises. The detailed work necessary to be informed on country conditions prior
to investment is exhaustive, but essential. For example, we outline
in the final chapter of this book some of the multitude of factors
that were researched in Tanzania prior to investment decisions by
the company with which we are associated, Sutton Resources Ltd.

Based on overall flows of foreign direct investments, the following list of countries highlights those that have been most popular with multinational corporations up to the start of the 1990s.

Australia	Germany	Singapore
Austria	Ireland	South Africa
Belgium	Italy	Spain
Canada	Japan	Sweden
Denmark	Malaysia	Switzerland
Finland	Mexico	U.K.
France	Netherlands	U.S.
Hong Kong	Norway	

Countries that have or will soon emerge as additional locations
for increasing volumes of foreign direct investment include:

Argentina	Hungary	Russia
Botswana	India	S. Korea
Brazil	Indonesia	Slovakia
Chile	Israel	Tanzania
Colombia	Ivory Coast	Thailand
China	Mauritius	Tunisia

Taiwan	Morocco	Turkey
Czech. Rep.	Namibia	Uruguay
Ecuador	Pakistan	Venezuela
Egypt	Peru	Vietnam
Ghana	Philippines	Zimbabwe
Greece	Poland	

Some of the countries on the above list may appear as surprising choices. Some, notably the poorer African nations, have been included because their fundamental economic reforms, which have barely been noted by international investors, will arouse rising global interest in the balance of this decade. Other countries on the list, such as the Russian Federation and Vietnam, have already aroused keen interest by investors, but not much actual flows of funds. These countries have been included here because they stand the chance of attracting vast investment amounts if they can introduce the right policies.

Size Influences Strategy

Large corporations have the resources for knowledge acquisition, but their very size may make them slow to act on new intelligence or so bureaucratic that good information fails to reach the right people. Some large corporations guard against this by attaching a very high value to obtaining new knowledge fast and having leaders with the courage to act quickly. Rupert Murdoch's News Corporation is an excellent example of this.

While many small and medium-sized enterprises may not have the funds to undertake in-depth global research and build knowledge models like Shell, they can often beat the major corporations by being faster and more flexible. If they can acquire good information and know how to use it efficiently, opportunities for them in the global market are vast. To be competitive, they must enter new foreign markets with all of the strength they can muster. Their top executives must be directly involved in obtaining information, travel often, and build their own crucial relationships. They must have the skills that enable them to gauge the accuracy of information brought to them by subordinates and potential business partners, and they must have the courage to act swiftly on new intelligence.

It has been our experience as investors to see an array of small, medium, and very large mining and minerals exploration companies send representatives to Africa. Some have failed to adequately research the cultural, historic, economic, and political conditions of the countries they have visited; some have solely focused on what their rivals are doing and on the geological attractiveness of the places they are visiting; and some have given the impression to us that they view almost all African countries as the same. In our own business in Africa we have just concentrated on Tanzania, and this has enabled us to constantly monitor economic and political developments in great detail and to develop excellent relationships in the public and private sectors through frequent and regular visits by our most senior executives. If we operated in several African countries at the same time, we would not have had the resources to accomplish this same level of information-gathering and contact development.

However, many of those who argue in favor of country diversification do so because they assert that it is the prudent course. What happens to your business if you just concentrate on one emerging economy and, subsequently, that economy becomes gripped by civil war or political leadership hostile to foreign business, is ravished by hyper-inflation that wrecks all cost projections, or experiences other similar disasters?

Our answer is that the investment of time, skilled experts, and money on the acquisition of knowledge can produce the depth of information from which real investment confidence springs. We believed, as a result of doing our homework, that we selected the most politically stable and hospitable country in Africa as the location for our investments. Our continuous updating of information has provided us with no evidence to suggest that we should change our perspective.

As emerging markets become of mounting interest to portfolio investors, corporations will need to demonstrate even more clearly that they have done their country selection homework and are absolutely well-informed on international developments. Portfolio investors will search for companies that demonstrate confidence based on solid facts in their foreign country choices. Shareholders will increasingly look for evidence that executives at their firms really know foreign markets and are able to maximize global opportunities.

Investors will go with corporations that clearly convey a sense of in-depth understanding of the politics, economics, and culture of the distant lands in which they are investing.

The investment in knowledge builds shareholder confidence and yields a direct financial return, quite apart from more obvious benefits. In the era of the new Industrial Revolution, more bankers, mutual fund analysts, and shareholders will be scrutinizing companies with regard to their global strategies, and the level of knowledge of their foreign investments that they demonstrate will be an acid test.

18

Building the Best Contacts

The knowledge needed to be successful in the boom era comes from a host of sources, but the most important source is other people. Finding the *right* people, the contacts who can provide solid, insightful information and leads, is one of the biggest headaches confronting corporate leaders today.

As corporations become increasingly multinational, the process of developing contacts becomes both more complicated and more time consuming for top management. To assist them in their searches, individuals inevitably develop networks of contacts—a group of people bound by similar profession, interest, geographic location, and so on. As business becomes more global, it is the analysis and the expansion of these networks that becomes crucial for success.

> "The most important source of knowledge is other people."

There are three general types of contact networks and concomitant sets of issues that are important in the global arena, each of which we will discuss in this chapter.

They are:

- Internal Contacts: Who should supply the strategic planning knowledge within a corporation, analyze it, and distribute portions of it to appropriate business divisions and top management?
- External Independent Contacts: Who should the corporation's leadership rely on in the international arena for accurate information, business leads, and for backing and support in joint ventures?
- External Institutional Contacts: With which external institutions, multinational and/or within the target country, should the corporation's leaders deal? On what terms and in which ways should these external contacts be used in order to maximize business opportunities?

Internal Contacts

For the individual business executive, the most critical contact networks are those that exist within the firm itself. As companies go global, internal networks become increasingly necessary to ensure that top managements are briefed on policies and developments shaping the international business environment. For example, core groups of in-house experts with knowledge of international opportunities help devise strategies that reflect full knowledge of the corporation's traditional business sectors and then present these strategies to top level decision makers. These core groups are comprised of individuals at corporate headquarters who are seen by managers around the globe as being repositories of knowledge and leads to other contacts.

> "The most critical contact networks exist within the firm itself."

Pooling together the in-house group of experts into an effective team that works closely with top management is the core of the essential organizational system. It is the critical factor in ensuring that knowledge and external contacts are bound together to yield precise, action-oriented options for corporate leadership decision making.

The in-house core group ensures that: the global strategic planning process is moving ahead; distinctions are being made between critically important knowledge and secondary information; effective evaluations can be made of the quality of external information sources and contacts; and other senior managers are kept informed on developments in the global process and are able to participate in it.

Building the in-house core contact team needs to be a top priority for corporate leadership when planning to go global. This is not easy, and frictions, not to mention "turf" wars, can easily surface between different corporate divisions as corporate top managements restructure their organizations to move from a largely domestic business focus to a fully global one. Thus, organizing to secure maximum advantage from knowledge acquisition can itself pose management challenges.

Some corporations have completely reshaped their top management structure to ensure a smoother transition to global operations. The members of the core group need to be team players. They need to be people who can blend well with the existing senior management team and not pose a new threat. At the same time, these individuals must have enough confidence to serve as effective critics and skeptics of the process without risking their careers or alienating their colleagues. They also need to be people who understand international finance, public relations, law, and human resources. The members of the core group represent the essential, internal contacts in the system—they are the people supplying the strategic planning knowledge within the corporation, analyzing it, and distributing it to the appropriate divisions and management within the organization.

The in-house team must also secure the appropriate balance between the use of internal executives and external contacts in the forging of strategic options. A situation in which long-serving senior executives see external experts as rivals must be avoided. Sometimes, the seasoned senior executive, who rose through the ranks because of his domestic business skills, starts to feel insecure as the corporation goes global. The outside expert who has evident knowledge of international markets can be intimidating. Sometimes external consultants exacerbate this feeling by highlighting their expertise and failing to recognize the degree of tension they are adding to their relationships with executives at the client corporation.

All too often, the temptation is to establish a special international division, or designate a senior executive as the Vice President, International. This is a mistake, as it immediately highlights distinctions between domestic and international operations, when in fact the maximum benefits will be derived from all parts of the company thinking and acting globally together. The correct approach is to ensure that top managers understand that their responsibilities have been broadened from the domestic base to a full, corporate overview that includes all international aspects. These top individuals, including the CEO, may then recruit experts with unique international experience who can broaden the existing management team, but not challenge and divide it.

In addition to being sources of information themselves, internal contacts also keep track of an expanding universe of external contacts. Top executives are broadening their contacts at a furious pace. Whereas, in the past, the chief financial officer might have relied on a local bank manager and, perhaps, an official from a leading money center bank, he or she now has a full network of investment banking contacts in financial centers around the world, as well as a complement of other financial contacts outside of the banking system (in cash management departments at other corporations, for example). The corporation's chief legal officer, who always used just a few outside law firms for corporate business, now has contacts in law firms around the globe. The bottom line is that in-house executives need to be fully included in the planning process and, within this context, in the search to secure excellent external contacts and knowledge.

Building the top team to transform a corporation is always difficult. Whether the corporation is downsizing in dramatic fashion or going global, change in the composition of the top management team is inevitable. The key in going global is to ensure that the transition is a plus sum game. Going international should not reduce the strengths of domestic business operations. Rather, it must enhance domestic business. From such understanding comes the ability to build the internal contacts who will provide the key inputs in the strategic planning process.

External Independent Contacts

The most important factor in searching for a local contact is that the individual must be trusted to provide solid, reliable information; he or she must be a genuine partner with the corporation and a participant in its local fortunes.

When the issue is finding prime local contacts in the most sophisticated and developed nations, the choices are substantial. In many European countries there are large numbers of eminent individuals for hire to multinational corporations. Often, they are retired civil servants and politicians. For example, many international corporations tried to hire Karl Otto Pôhl, the influential head of Germany's powerful central bank, when he announced his retirement several years ago. Then, to take another example, there was no shortage of proposals from private corporations flowing to Sir William Ryrie, who retired in 1993 from the chief executive post of the World Bank's private sector affiliate, the International Finance Corporation.

On the other hand, finding outstanding local contacts in developing countries is more difficult. For one, credentials mean less; in many countries the fact that someone once held a top political or civil service post is rarely an indication of their competence or knowledge. In these situations, individual referrals are the best method for securing excellent external contacts to assist with new market entry and corporate representation. These initial introductions may come from business in the target country, U.S. embassy officials, or World Bank representatives, to name a few. In turn, their referrals can lead to alliances with local business people who can become liaisons to local government and business.

Close association with local contacts—through equity joint venture partnership, retainer, or some other approach—is the safest means of checking information received from official sources, discovering which officials are important, and securing trustworthy local business people and organizations. The best local contacts expedite channels to important local sources of information and to the corridors of local power, thus ensuring that corporations meet with efficiency instead of bureaucracy.

It is all too easy to believe that there are substitutes for prime local contacts. Some common substitutes used by inexperienced corporations include executives from the businesses, associations, and chambers of commerce that proliferate in every country of the world. Some of these organizations are fronts for crooks, and others are nothing more than drinking clubs for old colonials. Although some of these organizations are effective, they can also be time-consuming diversions, and they are certainly not substitutes for effective local entrepreneurs willing to be strategic contacts.

Specialist Consultants

In searching for external specialists to augment in-house contacts, the key is not the specialist's discipline (increasingly in this highly competitive market they all provide similar services). Rather, the key is finding people who have genuine knowledge of the target countries. The consulting business seems to be growing by leaps and bounds. All manner of individuals—some made redundant from huge corporations that are downsizing, some forced into early retirement by investment banks that lost lots of money, and some who have just graduated from business schools—are offering services as international business experts. They are competing with individuals of outstanding experience. Selecting the right specialist is crucial, but getting the experience of consultants is essential.

As emerging markets become more important, some of the leading management consulting firms, auditing firms, and investment banks are strengthening their skills. There was a time when some of their executives professed a great deal more knowledge than they actually had, but competition and the growing importance of Third World business is forcing change. Companies are increasingly seeking to recruit people with excellent analytical skills and substantial experience in developing countries.

For example, the investment bank Morgan Stanley in New York recognized that China may play a central role in its fortunes in coming years and that, to ensure this, it had to go far beyond hiring a few Chinese specialists and housing them in offices in New York and in Hong Kong. Accordingly, it forged strategic alliances with a Chinese bank and with Asian investors to create a new bank in China, and it hired one of the world's leading experts to head this institution and be available to advise its clients. The man Morgan Stanley chose, Edwin Lim, had been the specialist economist on China for the World Bank in the first few years of China's membership in the institution in the early 1980s. Lim then became the World Bank's first resident representative in China. An American fluent in Chinese, he won exceptional respect from the top leadership of the Chinese Government; in fact, he was seen as a personal policy advisor to the country's leaders. In 1994, Edwin Lim left the World Bank for Morgan Stanley.

It is quite likely that investment banks will increasingly seek to hire staff from the World Bank, the International Monetary Fund, and other organizations that are home to excellent economists who are comfortable in the emerging economies—people who may not know much about business deals, but who can complement the skills of mainstream bankers with their profound analytical knowledge.

While the most prominent management consulting firms, auditing firms, and investment banks are preparing for the coming boom, the demands on them are far outweighing their resource skills. In this environment, the arena of geopolitical consultants has its full quota of charlatans: public relations firms that claim to know far more than they do; law firms whose knowledge of economics is confined to the ways they develop their client bills; and management consulting groups making exaggerated claims of their expertise in this area.

Among the better known of the specialist companies is Kissinger Associates. It is a small company, and its distinguished Chairman, Henry Kissinger, provides insights of considerable value that give comfort to chief executives of major corporations as they make large international business decisions. Former Secretary of State Henry Kissinger recognized early that, as increasing numbers of corporations sought to go global, CEOs would seek geopolitical advice and knowledge about their target countries and target regions of the world beyond that provided by their in-house staff. Dr. Kissinger appreciated that even if the CEO was comfortable with a major foreign investment decision, it would still have to be sold to the board. Kissinger's reputation and expertise combine to assist CEOs in selling major international decisions to their boards.

Kissinger Associates assists in this effort by providing well-researched political and economic analysis. Henry Kissinger's first partners were Alan Stoga, an excellent economist, Brent Scowcroft, and Lawrence Eagleberger. In the 1980s, when Scowcroft became head of the National Security Council and Eageleberger took a top State Department post (before eventually becoming Secretary of State), Kissinger invited J. Paul Bremer to join him as his chief analyst and deputy (Bremer had been U.S. Executive Secretary of State, Ambassador to the Netherlands, and Ambassador for Counter-Terrorism).

Kissinger Associates is almost a unique entity; its services are expensive, and it is busy. The alternative for many corporations who are seeking external assistance to better understand the rapidly changing global business environment is to search for outstanding individuals, rather than consulting firms, who know their stuff and are willing to admit their limitations. There are a small number of true experts around who, while admitting to limitations, know to whom they can turn for supplementary information. Finding these rare individuals is important. Corporate leaders who ignore this reality or skimp on the expense all too often make major geopolitical mistakes. Judgements must be formed within the local context. Knowledge of local traditions and conditions has to be carefully weighed with outside experts who have strong familiarity with the current local environment and its history.

External Institutional Contacts

Corporate decision makers must have confidence that the global business systems they are using are yielding outstanding data. That confidence derives from internal contacts, prime local contacts, and limited use of independent external professional contacts, especially when the focus is emerging economies. Confidence also derives from ensuring that the system has incorporated the views of a number of supplemental institutional contacts, whose organizations are storehouses of important facts, figures, and foreign contacts of their own.

The key here is to determine how a corporation can best use external institutional contacts. The lists of these institutions is getting longer as world trade and investment becomes ever more important. Business schools, think tanks, and business associations (such as the National Association of Manufacturers) are becoming increasingly valuable sources of basic information and analysis on emerging markets and the business opportunities that may exist there.[1]

In addition to these sources, there are two other types of external institutional contacts of considerable significance. These contacts are the international official organizations and the private international organizations.

International Organizations

On the international institutional front, the first ports of call for most multinational firms are the institutions belonging to the European Union, which are responsible for a market of over 350 million people. There are a number of these institutions, which are particularly headquartered in Brussels, but are also scattered across Europe, and they seem to grow by the day. For the most part, they are bureaucratic nightmares. They are home to some excellent people, but too often even the best talent is stifled by all manner of rules, regulations, and political in-fighting. The alternative, as an increasing number of multinational corporations

> "Developing direct access to key officials is a key strategy."

have discovered, is to develop means of direct access to key officials. Indeed, increasing numbers of firms have opened special Brussels offices, or engaged Brussels-based consulting firms to represent their interests.

Meanwhile, the United Nations produces more reports and statistics on emerging economies than anyone else. The focus of much of its work is on broad social and humanitarian issues and, while many U.N. agencies are home to individuals with excellent business understanding and knowledge, it can be an exhausting undertaking to try to find those people. In this book, we have relied on the work of the Division on Transnational Corporations and Investment of the United Nations Conference on Trade and Development for a lot of data and insights on multinational corporations. This small division at the Geneva offices of the United Nations produces work of exceptional quality.

The multilateral development banks today are developing increasing expertise in areas of private-sector Third World and Central and Eastern European development. The largest of these organizations is the World Bank, and the most important World Bank managers are those who direct the six regional divisions (Sub-Saharan Africa, the Middle East & North Africa, Eastern Europe & Central Asia, South Asia, East Asia, and Latin America & the Caribbean), each of which has a multibillion-dollar annual lending program. These managers all are based at the organization's headquarters in Washington, D.C., as are their departmental directors and key advisors. Access to them is generally straightforward and, indeed, it has been our experience that it is often easier to get telephone calls returned from top executives here than from the mid-level staff.

Many of the individuals at the World Bank have outstanding knowledge of the countries to whom they lend and the people who run those countries. These Bank executives are more objective in their perspectives than national officials, and most of them are approachable (unlike many of the economists across the street at the International Monetary Fund, who see their role as dealing solely with governmental officials). Today, the World Bank is seeking to expand the ways it can use its resources to catalyze private flows of funds to emerging economies. As it does this, its staff becomes increasingly interested in learning from corporate executives.

As the World Bank strives to find ways to strengthen the private sector in developing countries, its two major affiliates are becoming increasingly prominent: the International Finance Corporation, which, unlike the World Bank itself, can provide direct loans to corporations without government guarantees and also take equity positions, and the Multilateral Investment Guarantee Agency, which provides political risk insurance. Both of these organizations are intent on becoming more open to private sector inquiries and providing business with sound information.

More private sector directed policies are also increasingly evident at the leading regional development banks—essentially publicly owned, mini-World Banks: African Development Bank (Abidjan, Ivory Coast), Asian Development Bank (Manila, Philippines), Inter-American Development Bank (Washington D.C.), and the European

Bank for Reconstruction and Development (London). Businessmen are likely to find valuable information in these institutions, as well as in many of the smaller official regional development agencies around the globe.

Private International Organizations

A number of private international organizations that are also developing resources of value to corporations going global. Some of these resources can be found in the international business schools, such as INSEAD in France and the London Business School, which sponsor specialized conferences and have experts who may be useful to the corporate international strategist.

There are also exceptional private organizations that focus on global business which undertake their activities through conferences. The most famous of these organizations is the World Economic Forum (WEF), a Swiss organization that stages a major conference involving up to 2,000 participants in Davos, in the Swiss mountains, each February. WEF founder and president Klaus Schwab manages to assemble an impressive array of leading international politicians and business leaders in Davos each year. WEF also arranges numerous smaller conferences around the globe.

Then, there are a multitude of specialized organizations that focus on single sectors and have developed formidable research skills in those areas. These organizations range from institutions concerned with gold and precious metals, to those dealing with international finance, to others that concern themselves with almost every single specific business sector. Today, many of these international trade associations are striving to boost their membership by providing higher quality, more frequent international business information. They provide both source information, as well as competition to noteworthy international economic information companies, such as The Economist Intelligence Unit and Oxford Analytica.

As access to many of the official and private agencies with knowledge of global business conditions improve, and as these organizations produce ever more facts and figures and analytical reports, the issue of how the corporation organizes itself to take maximum advantage of available knowledge returns. We believe that with a strong arrangement of networks—internal contacts, external contacts, specialist consultants—and skills in accessing the international organizations, the entrepreneur and manager can gather and sort crucially needed knowledge in ways that lead to winning business decisions.

The trick then becomes how best to put the diverse elements of knowledge and contacts together to set the stage for positioning—for ensuring that new markets are approached the right way.

19

Positioning for Advantage

A corporation's reputation is its most valuable asset. To succeed in business in the era of the Industrial Revolution that we have described in this book, a corporation must establish a reputation of excellence on a global level, a reputation that secures respect, and, in turn, an advantage among its peers, employees, customers, suppliers, and sources of finance. How a corporation expresses its vision and its goals, indeed, how it acts in every emerging and traditional market it enters, is what new market positioning is all about. If this task is handled poorly, the corporation will lose business and tarnish its reputation.

> "A corporation's reputation is its most valuable asset."

Establishing an appropriate image (and, thus, a positive reputation) in a foreign country demands attention, because image influences the ways a corporation sells, builds relationships, secures resources, and negotiates the best deals. Sensitivity to perceptions of the corporation in new foreign markets is an essential factor in formulating the best new-market entry strategy. Entering the right way involves protecting the corporate reputation and establishing a local image of integrity.

Positioning the corporation on a global stage is becoming increasingly difficult, in large part because of the rising number of special interest organizations which monitor every possible type of activity undertaken by large firms. Activists, notably concerned with the environment or the plight of indigenous peoples in developing countries, are monitoring the actions of multinational corporations with vigilance and skill. Investors—individuals, pension funds, and other institutions—are also becoming sensitive to the growing diversity of global activities pursued by major enterprises.

As a result, corporations must take their positioning moves as seriously as a government's foreign office or state department takes the effective establishment of its diplomatic relations with foreign governments. In other words, positioning is now part of a complex and global strategy designed to forge new and effective relationships in ways that enhance prestige and influence, while, at the same time, minimizing risks.

> **"Positioning is a vital aspect of global strategy."**

Corporate positioning in a particular country must be in line with its overall global strategies. In this age of instant global news, no corporation can create one image for itself in one part of the globe and attempt to create a different image elsewhere. With increased telecommunications, a small mistake in one part of the multinational's far-flung empire will be immediately magnified into a disaster by the media. For example, a local manager of a U.S. corporation based in the Third World might be discovered seeking to pay a bribe to a local official. Within a few hours, this story would be reported in the *Wall Street Journal* and, as a result, shareholders will be influenced, the judgements of securities analysts will be colored, and the corporation's global image will be soiled. Remember, these repercussions resulted from the actions of one manager in one of the corporation's many foreign locations.

The global image of a corporation is the combination of decisions and actions taken at headquarters, combined with hosts of actions pursued in public view by the corporation's employees around the world. Therefore, a corporation must behave in each country in which it operates with sensitivity to its overall image. The way in which a business starts in a new market is crucial to the overall global image a corporation seeks to build. Once a corporation has done the work necessary to decide to enter a new economy, it must then focus on ensuring that it wins local respect. Although this is becoming an increasingly difficult task, the corporation must find elegant and dignified ways to stand out from the crowd and win greater goodwill than its rivals. There are several ways of achieving this important goal, including, but not limited, to involving top management in the effort, working with local media, using advertising and public relations to build goodwill, entering into joint ventures, and educating oneself about cross-cultural similarities and differences.

Involving Top Management

Corporate image is most influenced by top management. When the chairmen of Exxon or Ford, for example, visit an emerging economy, they are news; when they request an audience with a leader of an emerging economy, they get a positive response; when they publicly announce investment plans in an emerging economy, it causes intense, immediate interest in the economy's business community. Involvement of top management in the early phase of new market entry is of mounting importance in providing a firm with a positioning edge. At many corporations, top management is not seen in an emerging economy until the corporation's business has already been estab-

> "Involving top management in the early phase of new market entry can give a firm a positioning edge."

lished—at the end of the process, rather than at the beginning. This can prove to be a critical error.

In the new economic era, where more companies than ever before will be entering more foreign countries with a view to direct investment and long-term sales, the rewards will go to those that understand the importance of positioning. The competition in every emerging market, now and in the future, is so intense that no corporation has the luxury of time. When becoming established in new, emerging markets, much time can be saved by securing entry to the highest levels of government. With the right start, forged by top management with a country's public and private sector leaders, the company's staff can be among the first to obtain new business permits, learn of new government plans for the economy, and become aware of new government contracts and business opportunities.

Top management are often far better initial door-openers than are the mid-level management executives who have day-to-day responsibilities for the corporation's foreign expansion. These mid-level managers need to have the confidence to request top management participation in the early phase of new market positioning in emerging countries and this, in turn, is only created when top managers signal their interest in becoming active in the early new-market development efforts.

Extreme examples of how top managements took the first steps at new market positioning and enjoyed success are provided by the cola competitors. Pepsi-Cola had been a major supporter of Richard Nixon, and that connection proved an invaluable asset to the soda company in securing exclusive market rights for the Soviet Union. Pepsi Chairman Donald Kendall went with President Nixon to Moscow, ensured the Kremlin of his political influence, and achieved masterly new-market positioning. This lesson was not lost on its rival a few years later, when Jimmy Carter became President. Coca-Cola, a major supporter of Jimmy Carter, ensured its top management was very visible in the diplomatic arena, using its leverage to secure a monopoly for itself in China.

News Corporation is moving fast into emerging economies because its chairman, Rupert Murdoch, is directly engaged. He meets frequently with leaders of business and government in the countries that are his prime targets and, as he does so, he generates confidence in his vision. The losers in the new international economic game will be those giant corporations whose chairmen stay home because they believe they can compete with the Murdochs of this world by leaving positioning in new countries to staff technical experts.

Becoming Well Known

A critical issue in positioning, especially in emerging economies, whether in the Third World or in Central and Eastern Europe, is that nothing today can be taken for granted. Too often multinational corporations believe that they and their chairmen are better known outside of their home countries than they actually are. A corporate leader might be featured in *Business Week* magazine, or his firm may rank among *Fortune's* list of large U.S. enterprises, but from China to Zimbabwe, he and his corporation are likely to be unknowns.

Prudence dictates that, unless the company is a major multinational with a strongly promoted product brand name, such as Coca-Cola, American Express, IBM, Mercedes, or Shell, its management should assume that the company is unknown in most foreign countries. Western executives must also recognize that the fact that their corporations are large does not automatically mean that they will be welcome or enjoy advantages in emerging economies. In many countries, a giant multinational actually tends to have a negative image; multinationals are often portrayed by the media as having a will of their own, as being uninterested in adapting to local customs and sensitivities, and sometimes even as exploitative. On entering emerging economies, many Western companies need to ensure that such stereotypes do not prevail. This demands attention to contact development with local media and politicians at an early stage.

It is the arrogance of many of the largest multinationals and their lack of sufficient attention to general political positioning in the early phase of new foreign market entry that provides small- and medium-sized multinational corporations with unique opportunities. Smaller enterprises can be swifter on their feet, and their top executives can devote more time to developing contacts in new foreign markets. Establishing confidence with new and potential partners in emerging economies is central to corporate positioning. It is exhausting and hard to delegate, but it is also rewarding.

Working with the Media

In some cases, the initial efforts at new market entry need to involve attention to the local media, with the recognition that each country tends to have its own media traditions, habits, and ethics. For example, Americans often think that the British media operates with a similar value system to the U.S. media and that the continental European media follows the British lead. In reality, however, media approaches from the U.S. to Britain and from one European country to another are as different as chalk and cheese. A major difference is that, in the U.S., corporations do not pay expenses for reporters for fear they will be accused of offering a bribe. There is no way a *Wall Street Journal* reporter would accept airfare and hotel expenses to visit the foreign plant of a U.S. corporation. By contrast, many Western European journalists would not make the trip to see such a plant unless all expenses were paid by the inviting corporation.

Many multinational corporations underestimate the influence and the skill of the media in developing countries. For example, some of the most competitive and best journalists in the world are located in India. The *Hindu* of Madras, the *Economic Times*, the *Business Standard* in Bombay, and *India Today* are some of the first-class publications. And, as economic prosperity moves ahead and societies become politically more open, the media in the Third World is improving and becoming more of an independent force.

Too frequently, however, multinational corporations either fail to recognize this or believe that they can control the local foreign media. For example, while many U.S. corporations are now investing in India, few of them have made efforts to contact the influential Indian foreign correspondents based in the United States. This is an expensive oversight, because these foreign journalists can be most helpful in establishing a strong and positive reputation in their home country for U.S. firms. To avoid such errors, however, corporations need public relations staffs at their headquarters, as well as in the field, who are aware of the growing importance of the Third World's press. There are few multinationals that have media relations executives on staff who, like their CEOs, understand the importance of having a global state of mind and who are trained to be fully knowledgeable about the global media.

Those who so easily dismiss the Third World's media forget that it has frequently been courageous journalists and newspaper publishers who have challenged powerful political groups and dictators in developing countries and opened the eyes of the world to atrocities within these countries. For example, the first dramatic reports for international television on the drought in Ethiopia in the mid-1980s were produced, at great personal risk, by Kenyan journalist Mohammed Armin. This same journalist was again in the lead in reporting atrocities in Somalia in 1991.

In many countries, local editors and columnists are also sources of valuable information and insights on local conditions and can be helpful to new corporations seeking to position themselves. Most often, executives responsible for new market positioning are so intent on keeping a low profile that they fear contacting local media leaders. This is a costly error. It takes a great deal of time and patience to work with the local media in most countries, but candor and the willingness to educate can build trust.

The key to success is determining which are the best publications and identifying the experienced journalists of integrity within these publications. As emerging economies become more open societies, the media within them becomes more powerful. Understanding the media scene and knowing which journalists are most influential is a requirement for corporations seeking to position themselves in new markets. A few questions to a variety of local business people, government officials, and foreign diplomats

> "As emerging economies become more open societies, the media within them becomes more powerful."

usually produces a short list. From Argentina to Thailand and from Kenya to Pakistan, there are outstanding journalists, keen to learn, keen to recognize the value that the foreign investor represents, and keen to listen. Most frequently, the local press in these countries will welcome approaches from new foreign investors and act with intelligence and sensitivity.

Using Advertising for Emerging Market Entry

Advertising is another aspect of the Third World media that new investors need to understand and use in their positioning efforts. Some companies, most notably Coca-Cola, have effectively used advertising in their early new country positioning efforts, both for advertising their products and for advertising good community projects that they are supporting, such as local school soccer leagues and other sports events. In some countries, foreign companies that advertise in the early phase of their new market positioning are seen as having confidence and long-term country goals; these are attributes that win friends.

Quite a different aspect of advertising, which is increasingly common, arises when host governments approach new foreign investors to finance special newspaper and magazine campaigns in foreign countries to attract investment. Multipage supplements appear in *Newsweek, Institutional Investor, The International Herald Tribune,* the *New York Times,* and many other publications. All of the articles are paid for by the sponsoring governments. In turn, these reports are financed, at least in part, by advertising bought by foreign investors under moderate pressure from the host government. It is not always easy for a foreign company starting a business in an emerging country to refuse a direct request from the country's central bank governor or finance minister to pay for some foreign advertisements to assist the country's economy, but it is far from clear whether such outlays, which can be substantial, enhances the reputation of the corporation in the new foreign market or elsewhere.

Some of the special reports on countries in international publications that are sponsored by governments are quite good. However, many of them are of marginal value, devoting inordinate amounts of space to photographs of the head of state and leading politicians and containing articles that are full of glowing economic success stories that stretch credibility. The purpose of these reports is to promote the sponsoring country to the international community as a location for direct investment. Multinational corporations can more effectively use promotional funds to help governments achieve these goals without advertising in these questionable special reports. Taking a proactive stance here is just one approach to building goodwill in new markets.

Corporations can volunteer to directly assist the host government's foreign investment promotion efforts. By this means, the corporation demonstrates initiative, controls the budget for its outlays, shows that its work is effective, and wins significant goodwill with host governments. For example, Citibank strengthened its official relationships with the government of Pakistan in September 1992 by sponsoring a conference in New York at which Pakistan's leaders could directly promote their country to an audience of potential U.S. investors. The full-day session involved Pakistan's

Minister of Finance and Central Bank Governor, other top Pakistani officials, and an audience of over 500 U.S. business people. It was not difficult to convince senior officials from the International Monetary Fund, World Bank, and International Finance Corporation to come from Washington D.C. to New York to speak at the conference and lend a noteworthy air of credibility to the Pakistani claims of a new national strategy to welcome foreign investors.

The conference was worth several country advertising reports in assorted international publications for Pakistan, and, simultaneously, it effectively positioned Citibank vis-à-vis the Pakistani financial authorities at a time when its banking subsidiary in Pakistan was striving to take the lead on some key public sector contracts. In the battle between multinational corporations to stand out and win friends in the early phase of positioning in emerging economies, the type of initiative taken by Citibank in Pakistan has merit. Very few companies demonstrate such initiative, but, as the competition intensifies, more will have to. Moreover, this is a type of public relations activity that most corporations can easily undertake, but which most governments in emerging economies find very difficult to organize.

In addition to assisting with investment promotion, foreign corporations can take other imaginative actions to secure goodwill and build a positive reputation. Few corporations pursue these strategies, because, in large part, their executives in foreign countries do not have the interest, the terms of reference from their superiors, the experience, or the wisdom to undertake this type of effort. However, the costs can be small and the advantages significant. In this context, it is important to undertake actions outside of the glare of publicity. Assisting with multiyear commitments to good projects, without seeking to attract attention, does not go unnoticed. In time, top local officials will learn of what is being done, and they will not fail to openly express their thanks.

In many instances, the types of actions that secure long-term goodwill for the foreign investor involve social and environmental support programs. In the former, assistance might involve the rehabilitation of an orphanage, charitable contributions to voluntary welfare organizations, or programs in villages close to where the investing company is developing commercial interests. As for the latter, almost every foreign investor today can find an obvious involvement with the environment; few subjects are now as widely discussed or as politically sensitive. Investors can demonstrate environmental sensitivity by reaching beyond standard practice, becoming involved in supporting nongovernmental ecological groups and financing special projects. If the support is clearly long-term in nature, then it will be seen as sincere.

None of these actions is major, but the consistent, quiet support for initiatives in these areas contributes to the economic and social progress of host countries.

Building Contacts

In the previous chapter we highlighted the vital need to secure trustworthy, prime local contacts. Their skills are essential when a corporation entering a country for the first time as an investor seeks to swiftly build a positive reputation for itself. First impressions count for a great deal and are easily established, as executives from multinational corporations arrive in countries with which they are not familiar and seek to urgently establish their contacts with public officials (to secure work permits, register for business licenses, and so forth).

Determining the right officials can be difficult, because titles frequently have little meaning. Real power to act swiftly may rest in the hands of officials who do not have the largest offices. Often, it is important to make a wide array of contacts, including those among officials who carry political weight, even if their current areas of responsibility are remote from your own interests. If a prime local contact has been retained prior to making investments, then he or she will be able to ensure that the newly arrived executives from the U.S. or elsewhere do not waste time seeing the wrong officials or make mistakes because they are unfamiliar with local customs.

In most countries it is important for executives to build a wide network of governmental contacts. This can be a time-consuming activity in the first instance, but it can pay long-term dividends. Above all, it creates a strong reputation and earns respect. Some foreign corporations make the mistake of narrowly defining the range of local political and official contacts in new foreign markets. They restrict themselves to contacts that have a precise relationship to their businesses, such as ministries of customs and labor and the foreign exchange divisions of finance ministries and central banks. This is fine from a day-to-day working perspective, but it is insufficient if the corporation is to achieve rapid action on its plans and secure longer-term expansion and development. Foreign corporations need to learn about the political structures in the countries they are entering and ensure that top governmental officials know and respect them.

Joint Ventures

A crucial positioning question for every newcomer to an emerging economy today is whether it should start on its own or seek a strategic alliance of some kind with already established businesses in the country. Joint ventures take many forms and are, in effect, designed to provide each participant with a distinct set of benefits. So long as these benefits remain mutual, the alliance can thrive.

Giant firms, such as IBM, have scores of alliances around the world, most of which involve no equity relationship but are distinct types of limited partnership agreements. Managing strategic alliances can be time-consuming, and many entrepreneurs have found that, over time, the effort is so great that they would be better off by flying solo. But upon reaching such a conclusion, they have already achieved their first goals: they have entered a new market and achieved effective initial positioning within it.

For many firms, the road to reaching that positioning objective is through formation of some kind of joint venture with an existing local partner. Issues related to forming joint ventures, including such topics as market access, trust, and control, are increasingly becoming hot themes at business schools.

It is almost impossible for a foreign enterprise to effectively secure a significant foothold in a business sector in numerous countries, including the former Soviet Union, without having a local partner. In time, this fact may change, but as long as the economic situation is lacking in effective regulation, it will be prudent for the foreign investor to join with experienced local interests.

With regard to trust, the focus for foreign investors has to be on the character of the partner, rather than on the legal nature of alliance language. If the partner proves to be a crook, then signed legal agreements are unlikely to be of much help. It is amazing how many corporations select joint venture partners quickly and with a minimum expenditure of resources and then spend quite heavily on the very best lawyers to ensure the agreement looks as if it protects the investor from all possible contingencies.

Joint venture partners can be found through a range of mechanisms, including soliciting the expertise of local sponsors, requesting information from government authorities, seeking information at the local chamber of commerce and at local banks, and securing support and guidance from international organizations. As with establishing contacts, investing in the search for good people is vital.

Control within joint ventures is a complicated issue, especially in emerging economies and in Central and Eastern Europe. Too much can be made of equity control in the form of ownership of 51 percent of the shares in a joint venture. It is quite possible for an international company to be the minority shareholder in a joint venture and still have critical control because it is the sole foreign exchange supplier; it controls patents, technical, and managerial know-how, or it controls the international marketing of the products produced.

Control tends to be reflected in the details of legal agreements concluded between the partners rather than in the shareholding structure of a local entity. Transparency in the affairs of a new venture is more important than share ownership control. The most successful joint ventures are those in which there is:

- Agreement between all participants on the goals and strategies;

- Systems for continuous, easy communications between the partners;

- Distinct awareness among all individuals involved of cultural and traditional differences that may influence individual communications and working relationships;

- Clarity in contracts over the roles and responsibilities of each partner; and

- Written, contingent understandings of how to dissolve the joint venture and divide assets should this become necessary.

Negotiating

When you are starting to find your feet in a new market, you face the most serious of all initial positioning tests—entering into negotiations. For example, companies may negotiate to secure a mining agreement from the government, to forge a joint venture with local investors, or to acquire a local business. How the negotiations end is clearly of immediate significance for your corporation's bottom line, and the way in which the negotiations are conducted has a major influence on corporate reputation.

We have worked alongside Dr. Roman Shklanka, Vice-Chairman of Sutton Resources, Ltd., and have the highest regard for his negotiating skills. Dr. Shklanka has been negotiating mining deals around the globe for many decades. His approaches have not only yielded excellent immediate business outcomes for the companies with which he has worked (he was a senior executive of Canada's Placer Dome Inc., one of the world's largest mining companies, before joining the Board of Directors of Sutton in the late 1980s), but they have also resulted in establishing excellent local relationships for these companies. His work has enhanced the reputations of the companies he has represented, and he has demonstrated how important negotiation can be for international market positioning.

We could not agree more with the sage advice Dr. Shklanka provided at a mining industry conference in British Columbia in October 1994, in a detailed paper titled "Negotiating Internationally With Governments." In short, Dr. Shklanka said that international negotiations amount to negotiating between cultures. He stated:

> In order to be effective internationally, you need to understand the contents of your own cultural baggage, need to learn as much as possible about the cultures with which you are working, and need to develop an international cultural perspective of the way things may be different abroad when compared with your own culture.

He also noted that:

> To be effective globally does not require memorizing all the do's and don'ts that apply to each country, but, rather, the development of an international mind-set. This is developing a feel or approach to doing business with associates whose cultural orientation differs from your own so that the differences do not undermine negotiations.

Dr. Shklanka outlined ten basic, cross-cultural ground rules:

1. Values, like the different cultures they are part of, are not negotiable.

2. Cross-cultural information is not about being more like them or them more like you. People cannot be who they are not, with nothing more damaging to a relationship than inauthenticity. The information is to help you adjust to expectations about preventive action and is ultimately about increasing your options through learning from them.

3. The most disruptive cross-cultural problems tend to emerge over deep cultural misunderstandings rather than over specific behavioral differences. Differing concepts of time will affect how quickly the negotiation moves along; notions of socializing in business will determine the emphasis placed on developing relationships; beliefs regarding hierarchy, status, age, and position will determine the style and content of protocol; beliefs regarding sex roles will affect the power and presence of both men and women.

4. Through attribution, that is, the projection of our own values onto the behavior we perceive in individuals of other cultures, we might account for what they do according to our standards, instead of matching their behavior against the standards of their own culture. For example, we may see Arabs or Latin Americans who stand too close to us as aggressive, rather than normal to their culture; we might interpret the East Indian looking away as an intent to avoid, when it is actually a sign of respect.

5. Through selecting out, we may recognize familiar behavior, but are less likely to recognize or correctly interpret unfamiliar behavior. For example, Singaporeans, like most Asians, place a great emphasis on 'saving face,' so that, despite their apparent directness, forthrightness, and speed of response, they may be slow to deliver bad news.

6. Ethnocentrism, the belief that one's own culture is central, is one of the biggest threats to negotiating internationally. It denies the respect others are due, it

breaks down communication by generating anger and resentment, and it keeps people from the truth about one another.

7. There are only a few things you can do about language differences. If you can afford to bring an interpreter, then bring your own. Interpreters who convey meaning are preferred to translators who simply translate the words from one language into another. If your interpreter understands your needs, he is more likely to provide you with the information you want. Recognize that most people will break into their own language at negotiations not to hide something, but because it is easier to communicate among themselves. Speaking the same language does not ensure similarity in culture and can be deceptive. When English is spoken and is not the first language, reply in simple terms, speak slowly, avoid colloquial expressions or words with more than one meaning, and confirm understandings.

8. Remember that differences are not necessarily cultural. They may be environmental, individual peculiarities, or corporate attitudes.

9. Discomfort, displeasure, unease, fatigue, and disorientation are all common international business side effects. So, keep a sense of humor and adventure. Prepare, and be rested and ready.

10. In international business, the relationship is perhaps the single most important aspect to consider. In most other cultures, a relationship must be established as a prerequisite to doing business; in our environment, this prerequisite is an anomaly.

Positioning is a critical component of strategy for any multi-national corporation, large or small. In the boom period ahead, when more and more international firms seek to become full-scale multinationals, the challenge for many of them will be to make a distinct, positive name for themselves at the outset in new markets. Above all, they must find ways to stand out from the crowd.

If multinational corporations have invested in knowledge and building contacts and if they understand that the chief corporate executives must be directly engaged in positioning efforts, then they may be successful.

20

Practicing What We Preach

Business leaders are usually ahead of politicians, academics, and the media in envisioning new trends, seeing new markets developing, and recognizing that whole new global industries can be created that will change international relations. While many people in other professions may still hesitate before accepting the proposition of a new Industrial Revolution, those in business are investing vast sums in new global strategies—strategies that will only pay off if there is a sustained period of unprecedented global economic growth.

Business is the driving force behind the development of the increasingly integrated European Union, the U.S.–Canada–Mexico trade agreements that will open the door to a broader set of economic liberalization arrangements throughout the Western Hemisphere, and other efforts to integrate the world's economy. Business has developed the 24-hour market for currencies, commodities futures, securities, and almost all other traded instruments that recognize no national borders. Business has also built a huge, rapidly expanding capital market open to increasing numbers of emerging economies.

National governments in the most developed industrial countries have often voiced concern about these global financial developments, seeing in them possible threats to the stability of financial institutions and to the world's economic stability. However, these governments have grudgingly recognized that they lack the powers to roll-back the forces of global economic interdependence that businesses are promoting. As companies plan global communications, for example, they design systems to communicate with literally every individual on the planet. To do this demands joining together talents and technologies now found in a range of distinct ' businesses—marketing, entertainment, electronics, computers, and telecommunications. Would it be absurd to envision a day when CNN forged a global alliance with Microsoft, WPP, AT&T, and other giant enterprises? Not at all.

Creative Confusion

While governmental antitrust regulators still think of monopolies in terms of single industries, today's global entrepreneurs consider merging whole industries into new constellations on a universal scale. Confusion is raging in the business world, as new technologies come on stream to create whole new ways of thinking about business linkages and as rapid growth in the developing countries opens broad vistas of new marketing opportunities. The confusion is a positive, creative force, especially for the most imaginative companies. It forces us to search for original strategies with an ever-expanding number of variables, permutations, options, and opportunities.

To those who invest in multinational corporations, the confusion is also profound. Increasingly, their companies are undertaking a wider range of businesses, entering a rising number of strategic alliances with other corporations, and moving into an ever-growing number of countries. Where once the traditional telephone company was firmly anchored to its singular effort in the United States, it now talks about its future in China and India and its entry into the entertainment business. The multibillion dollar joint venture announced in Spring 1995 between MCI and News Corporation underlines this point. Meanwhile, computer manufacturers toy with direct challenges to the telecommunications giants.

In this age of creative confusion, Coca-Cola, while searching for a new marketing approach in 1993, went far beyond the world of traditional advertising agencies and hooked up with Creative Artists Agency, a Hollywood talent agency which has subsequently been responsible for dozens of Coca-Cola advertisements. Many people in the advertising business were stunned, just as they were when, in that same year, Sony chose its own entertainment subsidiary, Sony Pictures, rather than its traditional advertising firm, to produce its advertisements. Did this mean that filmmakers were about to take over the mass marketing arena?

These examples represent only the tip of the iceberg. Just as entertainment companies are starting to crowd advertising agencies, the competition among the entertainment companies themselves is increasing. Global giants have been formed and are now forming to market music, CD-Roms, videos, and even theme parks. The biggest global players in this business, as of mid-1994, were: Matsushita Electric Industrial (MCA) and Sony of Japan; Bertelsmann of Germany; News Corporation of Australia; and Walt Disney, Time Warner, Viacom/-Paramount, Capital Cities/ABC, TCI and CBS, all of the United States.

Never before have corporations in so many countries monitored businesses in other countries and in other industries as closely as they do today. There is an increasing sense in business around the globe that whole new industries are evolving and that traditional firms are literally changing their focus as they exchange a national coat for a global one. Technology is driving much of this change.

A Place for Small Business

The expanding international market is not confined to large enterprises alone. The Japanese are again ahead of everyone else here. Japanese small- and medium-sized enterprises (SMEs) are rapidly expanding their direct foreign investments. The United States is the single most popular investment location, but the Japanese SMEs are also giving increasing priority to investment in the developing economies of South and East Asia.[1]

Regardless of their home location, many SMEs experience a natural resistance to the suggestion of operating overseas. They feel that any such initiative will be a burden on their already limited managerial and financial resources. In addition, they believe that any deviation of their attention from their main market might be regarded as the realm of large transnational corporations and, therefore, be outside of their own capabilities. Such attitudes may be further reinforced by the negative beliefs about operating in developing countries because of the greater difficulties and risks. These are prejudices that will increasingly be dispelled.

A United Nations' survey of small- and medium-sized enterprises around the world found that there are four main areas in which SMEs can enjoy competitive advantages over large transnational corporations in the international arena:

- They take advantage of production opportunities left open by large companies (niche production);

- They may possess technologies that have been phased out by large firms (mature technologies), but for which there remain distinct markets;

- They have advantages in downscaling technologies to small markets, in making production more labor intensive, and in adapting to local factor proportions; and,

- They can gain cost advantages by having highly flexible and simple organizational structures—in fact, flexibility of management represents SME's greatest source of competitive advantage.

Boom in Action: Our Own Story

These factors, combined with the arguments outlined throughout this book, have been the driving force behind our own investments. We, too, are taking advantage of the new Industrial Revolution, and we expect to profit from the coming boom. If the judgements and perspectives we have outlined in this book are wrong, then it will not be difficult for the public at large to see the results. The acid test will be the evolution of Sutton Re-sources Ltd.[2]

> "Deflation and massive restructuring of Third World economies will set the stage for a new era."

Sutton did not enter emerging economies until the late 1980s and, when it did, it entered countries that were not attracting significant investor interest: Tanzania in East Africa and Guyana in Central America. In fact, at that time, Sutton was almost alone among new foreign investors entering these countries, but, today, both are most definitely on the map for mining companies around the globe that are searching for new opportunities.

As we have discovered in Tanzania, for example, where the great majority of Sutton's activities are concentrated today, being among the first international investors and taking great pains to position well has yielded benefits for Sutton. Tanzania is an economically underdeveloped country, which, like most African countries, has not been on Wall Street investment screens. Most private sources of international finance have been content to leave the financing of the governments of these countries to official organizations like the International Monetary Fund and the World Bank.

Developing a Vision and Strategy

Sutton's success owes much to a major investment of time by its top executives to understand these countries, see the opportunities they can offer, and position the company to take advantage of some of these opportunities. The idea to develop a Canadian minerals exploration company into a major player in the global mining of precious and base metals had its origins in an analysis of global market demands for metals.

We were, and we remain, convinced that the deflation introduced in the early 1980s as a response to the double-digit inflation of the 1970s, coupled with forced, massive restructuring of Third World economies, will set the stage for a new era of prosperity. We also believed, and we continue to believe, that the global market for base and precious metals will rapidly expand as a result of this growth.

Data to support this perspective developed as the 1980s progressed and provided the underpinning for Sutton's vision: to maximize shareholder value by becoming a major producer of the critical metals we determined will be in demand in the latter part of the 1990s, as the emerging economies of the world move into sustained levels of high growth.

Sutton's approach is based on the calculation that the dawning of a new economic era will bring exceptional rewards to those companies that have good managers in place, have acquired excellent knowledge of global trends, are located in stable and outward-oriented countries that respect foreign investors, and that control major mineral resources. Having set its corporate vision and strategy, Sutton then needed to bring together the combination of highly skilled people, the right choice of metals, and the right country selections for locating and mining the metals.

Finding the Right People

In the latter part of the 1980s, Sutton was a small company engaged in minor ventures in North America. The company needed capital to partner with Roman Shklanka, the recently retired head of exploration at Placer Dome Inc., who wanted assistance in exploring a range of foreign minerals prospects. Shklanka had extraordinary international experience and, with Placer Dome, had already established a minerals exploration venture in Tanzania, developed contacts there, and acquired knowledge about the nation's mineral resources.

Our contribution at this stage was to build Sutton's capital base and, therefore, the means for attracting Shklanka to the Sutton team, and to open the way into foreign countries. Among the most interesting prospects brought to Sutton's attention were a potentially large nickel deposit at Kabanga, in the Kagera Region in northwestern Tanzania, a gold deposit in the Marudi Mountain area of Guyana, and a large gold deposit at Bulyanhulu, in Tanzania. Nickel, cobalt, and gold were assets that directly meshed with the basic, driving vision of rising natural resources prices.

Country Selection

Sutton's next critical strategic issue became country selection. The fact that a country might have superb undeveloped minerals was not sufficient. There also had to be a sense of confidence that the political and economic environments would be hospitable over the long term for Sutton. Detailed knowledge of the countries was essential. Shklanka, who had experience in both countries, found excellent individuals—Maurice Hamilton in Guyana and William Bali in Tanzania—to provide contacts and country knowledge. Hamilton and Bali are prime local contacts, whose involvement allowed us to attain our goal of securing a team of first-class people.

Knowledge of Guyana was less difficult to secure than that concerning Tanzania. Guyana is small, with a population of less than one million, but it has been highly dependent on Canadian and U.S. multilateral development assistance, and there has been an increasing amount of gold exploration taking place in the country and in nearby Venezuela by a variety of corporations.

Tanzania was different. It is a very large country, with a population of over 27 million, that has a very low average per capita income. From independence in 1961 to the mid-1980s, Tanzania had a socialist government that made foreign investment difficult. Though it had changed its policies, this was not well known in the late 1980s. When Sutton started its research, few foreign companies had made significant new investments. Although data published by United Nations geologists in the 1970s showed that Tanzania had very large nickel–cobalt deposits, no work had been done on these deposits in the 1980s.

As the government announced significant changes in its economic policies in the late 1980s, it was apparent to those who spent time learning about the country, its people, and its politics that this would emerge as an outstandingly hospitable environment for foreign direct investment. Sutton determined that if all the information it could amass was favorable, then it would be beneficial to position the company to ensure that it was fully welcome in the country and could enjoy the new opportunities that would arise as Tanzania increasingly attracted foreign investment.

Sutton determined that Tanzania was the right country in which to concentrate investment. Had other companies done similar research at the time, they would have very likely reached similar conclusions, and Sutton would have had much greater competition. But Tanzania was not on the trendy lists at investment banking houses, and there was little news circulating in the media about Tanzanian developments. In some cases in the early 1990s, we even encountered U.S. bankers who claimed to be global natural resources experts, but who had either never heard of Tanzania or were not interested in it.

Why We Selected Tanzania as the Key Location for Our Foreign Investment

Sutton determined to invest in Tanzania after a lot of study and after finding that the country enjoyed the critical attributes that a mining company should demand in making a country selection:

- An attractive natural resource base;
- Historic political stability;
- A common language and high literacy level throughout the country;
- Negligible tribal or ethnic problems;
- Natural geographical advantages (ports, rail, roads, air links);
- Climatic advantages;
- Western aid support for vital infrastructure financing;
- Exceptional economic reform track record since mid-1980s;
- Economic policies backed by the International Monetary Fund;
- Evolutionary development of political institutions towards democracy and free market systems;
- Welcoming attitude to foreign investors;
- Clear legislative framework for foreign investors;
- Political understanding of the special needs of extractive industries;
- Rational tax policy and competitive incentive systems;
- Realistic ecological requirements;
- Capable and honest officials in top government positions; and,
- A positive governmental approach to negotiations, with government support for and participation in international conventions governing insurance of foreign private assets and the international arbitration of business disputes.

In addition to the positive signs we uncovered in our research, we also visited extensively with officials and the people of the country. Sutton executives worked with the Ministry of Energy, Water, and Minerals and negotiated agreements that enabled Sutton to start exploration work in Kagera. Those negotiations, conducted in an open and fair manner,[3] contributed to setting the stage for Sutton's expanding investments in the country. All of our experiences attested to the honesty and fairness of the people and to their serious interest to operate in a meaningful, partnership fashion with investors willing to make a genuine, long-term investment commitment. We understood that it was up to us to forge relationships and build goodwill for the long term.

Building Relationships

At the same time Sutton started exploration operations and negotiated an initial permit for this purpose, we made it clear to the leaders of the Tanzania government that our commitment to Tanzania was intense in personal as well as corporate terms. Frequent visits were made to the country for the express purpose of assisting the government and local communities in areas that had nothing to do with mining, but everything to do with the country's future prosperity. Every effort was made to ensure that all of the assistance was given with total transparency, as we were all well aware that our business successes in the country would inevitably create jealousies that could all too easily spawn rumors of corrupt practices. We consider it essential, in terms of our personal reputations, the image of Sutton, and the standing of all of the people we deal with in Tanzania, to ensure that integrity is visibly at the forefront of all our actions. Directors of Sutton have provided (and continue to provide) technical assistance to the government in many of its investment promotion activities: designing, developing, and publishing booklets for the government; arranging for ministers to participate in international business conferences; providing information to ministers for general international investment speeches; and securing international press coverage for the government's pro-investment policies.

Sutton provided these services because it recognized that the overall environment for private business in the country would be enhanced by the attraction of increasing numbers of foreign investors, even rival mining houses, and, thus, these actions were explicitly in Sutton's own interest. Sutton's activities enabled it to learn more about the political and economic systems, while being seen as useful to the country's future. [4]

This effort at positioning in Tanzania was only possible because of the personal engagement of Sutton's senior managers and directors; they repeatedly demonstrated to the government that Sutton was a company which understood that its success would also be Tanzania's success and that fair partnership was the way ahead. This has bought respect and trust, the crucial ingredients for long-term corporate success.

Companies much larger than Sutton have entered Tanzania in recent years, but few have enjoyed as good a relationship with business and government. Most have gone about country entry in the traditional manner, sending in the technical people first and demanding actions by the authorities. Some have acted with great arrogance in Tanzania and elsewhere in the Third World, making unrealistic demands that highlight their insensitivity and ignorance. Sutton's investment in positioning taught it about the Tanzanian way of doing things, about the timeframes that have to be expected for different kinds of official actions, and about the appropriate ways to behave to secure a real partnership.

Taking on a Partner

The initial nickel and cobalt exploration in 1990 and 1991 uncovered one of the world's largest undeveloped nickel belts; the Kagera Region is rich in nickel, cobalt, and copper. Negotiations were undertaken with the government to expand Sutton's exploration area, and, in mid-1992, this resulted in an agreement covering 10,000 square miles. So exceptional were the initial exploration results from Sutton's drilling in Tanzania that the company determined it needed a major partner to fully proceed with the project. Several of the largest mining houses showed interest, and an agreement was signed with BHP Minerals International Inc., a division of BHP Australia, that country's largest industrial company and one of the world's top three mining firms.

As Sutton moved ahead in Tanzania, it became evident that there were a variety of other attractive minerals exploration opportunities in the country. Sutton's success and the joint venture with BHP, as well as the policies introduced by the government, resulted in rapidly increasing interest in Tanzania by international mining companies. By mid-1994, more than 100 applications from international mining companies for various types of mining permits were being reviewed by the government.

Sutton was especially interested in a substantial gold prospect that, as of the 1980s, had been worked at times by both a mining consortium from Finland and by Placer Dome, whose data indicated substantial gold reserves. In 1994, Sutton concluded a major agreement with the government covering this prospect. We believe Sutton was selected not only because it offered competitive commercial terms, but also because it had demonstrated over the previous four years that it was committed to Tanzania's development. The Tanzanians knew that Sutton would keep its word and invest major sums in new ventures. In short, it could be trusted.

Reaping the Rewards

This approach in Tanzania yielded good results for all parties. It represents the form of partnership that we believe is essential for Western firms to adopt as they enter emerging economie now and in the future. We believe that our method can bring rich rewards and that many aspects of our approach should be replicated by other firms entering the emerging economies. These countries are the future great growth markets, and many of

> "Going global is no longer a matter of choice."

them are led by politicians who are sophisticated and who understand the prospects ahead as well as the ways of international firms. They are led by people who are just as willing to do deals with small- and medium-sized corporations as with large ones, if the deals are based on trust, long-term commitment, and sincere partnership.

We believe that the successful businessmen and women in the next decade will be those who understand the dynamics of international economic and political relations and who approach the international arena with a conceptual recognition of the vital need to adopt a partnership approach. This approach is working for us in our Sutton adventure, and it will work for others.

This is an approach that most companies will have to learn, because going global is no longer a matter of choice. The decision to expand from a domestic base into the international arena is compelling for entrepreneurs and investors engaged in almost every sector of the economies of the most developed industrial countries today.

Increasing numbers of today's business leaders are reaching their lofty heights in large corporations because of their successes in international markets. More and more companies are recognizing that talented individuals of all nationalities deserve great opportunities in multinational companies. It is familiarity with the world arena that will increasingly become a minimum requirement for promotion to the top echelons of business.

These experienced business leaders are the actors who are filling growing roles on a stage that already is full of bright lights. The script is being written in recognition of the reality that there is no precedent for the type of genuinely global economic boom, with all of its inevitable political ramifications, that is being unleashed by the dawning of a new Industrial Revolution. The curtain is about to go up on a century that will see levels of global business integration and activity that dwarf those that are now visible.

There are few virgin business territories left, as whole areas of the globe are being transformed. Vast new markets are being created. Many businesses may fail in their efforts to develop in the most difficult and most remote corners of the new global economy, but each failure will be a pioneering move, adding to total business experience and knowledge and paving the way, perhaps, for eventual business successes in the same areas.

The New Era of Prosperity

Never before have world markets been so exciting. They offer great yields, and still greater ones may be in prospect, as all markets become more linked by finance, telecommunications, computer technologies, and multinational investors. Information is the critical currency that will create a still more hectic tempo of developments in the remainder of the 1990s, setting the stage for a new century.

In the 21st century, more people will travel across national borders and transact more international business than any of us today can possibly imagine. More people than ever before will come to enjoy decent and rising living standards in the era of prosperity that is about to dawn. It is an era which will contain the wealth, and perhaps the wisdom, to secure a more peaceful world—a world where far fewer people are denied the basic human rights of decent food, shelter, health services, clothing, and educational opportunities that can lead them to bring hope and comfort to their families and their communities.

Notes

Chapter One

1. The Organization for Economic Cooperation and Development (OECD) has estimated that if China, India, and Indonesia grow by an average of 6 percent a year (and currently they are showing even higher average growth), and their income distributions remain unchanged, by 2010 some 700 million people in these countries—roughly equal to the current combined populations of the U.S., Japan, and Western Europe—will have an average income equal to that of Spain today, as compared to 100 million people at present in these three developing countries. The OECD is an international organization, based in Paris, France, whose members are the governments of the 26 most advanced industrial countries and which provides its members with a forum for economic policy coordinating discussions and economic analysis.

2. *The Economist*, October 1, 1994.

3. Estimates here and in following pages on population, food consumption and education levels in different parts of the world come from an address by Gautam S. Kaji, Managing Director of the World Bank, at the Conference on Sustainable and Equitable Development, in Canberra, Australia, in March 1994, from reports published by The World Bank, notably *World Development Report 1993,* and *World Development Report 1994,* published by Oxford University Press, and from the United Nations Development Programme (UNDP) studies, notably *Human Development Report 1994,* published by Oxford University Press.

4. An in-depth look at education in Tanzania is provided by Lene Buchert in "Education in the Development of Tanzania: 1919-1990" published by Ohio University Press in Athens, James Currey in London, and Mkuki na Nyota in Dar es Salaam.

5. The development of "super rice" and numerous other brilliant agricultural breakthroughs that have changed Third World food prospects are often funded by the Ford Foundation, Rockefeller Foundation, other philanthropies, and the member research institutes around the world of the Consultative Group on International Agricultural Research (CGIAR), together with technical assistance secured through official foreign aid.

6. Breakthroughs and intense cooperation between Merck pharmaceutical company, the World Health Organization, and the World Bank have created a safe era where once "river blindness" reigned supreme in West Africa.

7. Technology is creating a global "borderless economy," suggests Fumio Sato, President and Chief Executive Officer of Toshiba Corporation of Japan in a Toshiba advertisement in the *Financial Times,* June 27, 1994.

8. Mr. Craig McCaw and William Gates announced the formation of Teledesic Corporation on March 21, 1994, as reported in the *Wall Street Journal* of that day, *The Economist* of March 26, 1994, and *Newsweek* of April 4, 1994.

9. Milton Friedman, article in the Hong Kong-published *Far Eastern Economic Review,* October 28, 1993.

10. Milton Friedman, article in the Hong Kong-published *Far Eastern Economic Review,* October 28, 1993.

11. The G7, Group of Seven, consists of the United States, Canada, France, Germany, Italy, United Kingdom, Japan, and Canada. The government leaders of these countries hold an annual

225

summit—the most recent was held in Halifax, Nova Scotia, in June 1995—and the G7 Finance Ministers meet several times each year.

12. Comments in 1994 by Malaysia's Finance Minister following disclosures in the British press about actions by the Government of Mrs. Margaret Thatcher in 1988 to win defense contracts from Malaysia and, in conjunction with this, provide Malaysia with development aid for a clearly uneconomic dam project. The press, while seeing the former Thatcher Government as its target, described the Government of Malaysia as corrupt.

13. See Chapter 10 and the 1994 and 1995 newsletters of Transparency International, the not-for-profit organization established to curb corruption in international business transactions.

14. The General Agreement on Tariffs and Trade (GATT) was established 50 years ago to provide mechanisms for governments to negotiate treaties to increase trade between nations. The most recent of these treaties, involving more than 100 countries, was completed in 1994 and was known as the Uruguay Round, as the negotiations were launched in 1986 at a conference in Uruguay. Not only did the 1994 treaty reduce barriers to trade for scores of products and services, but it replaced GATT with a new World Trade Organization (WTO), based in Geneva, Switzerland and designed to be a most vigorous enforcer of international free trade arrangements. In addition to the recent GATT agreement, the momentum for global growth through expanded trade has been assisted with some major new regional trade treaties: for example, the North American Free Trade Agreement between Canada, the U.S., and Mexico, and, as another example, the expansion of the European Union, as more nations have joined this common market.

15. Professor Paul Krugman writing in the July/August 1994 *Harvard Business Review*.

16. Barings, one of the oldest of British merchant banks, collapsed under massive losses from derivatives transactions in Spring, 1995 and was acquired by the ING banking group of the Netherlands. For "Baring's best buys," see *Forbes*, July 4, 1994. That internal management controls were less than sound at the 233 year old bank became evident as investigations were pursued in 1995—see, for example, story by Nicholas Brady in the *Wall Street Journal*, July 7, 1995.

17. In early 1995, the U.S. Treasury led global efforts to aid Mexico, with the U.S. government's Exchange Stabilization Fund being pledged to the tune of $20 billion and the International Monetary Fund agreeing to provide a further $17.8 billion.

18. Comments by George V. Grune, Chairman and, until 1994, Chief Executive Officer of the Reader's Digest Association, Inc., in the keynote speech to The Conference Board's 1990 Marketing Conference.

Chapter Two

1. See Global Trends Chapter, *World Investment Report 1994*, published by United Nations Publications, and written and edited by the Division on Transnational Corporations and Investment of the United Nations Conference on Trade and Development.

2. 1993 Annual Report, The Coca-Cola Company, Chairman's Message to Share Owners, titled, "A Global Growth Company."

3. On Ogilvy & Mather Worldwide's winning of the exclusive global IBM contract, *Advertising Age*, reporting the story on May 30, 1994, started by declaring, "It was the marketing shot heard 'round the world, and more than 40 agencies ended up taking the bullet."

4. Statement by Lester Korn at the 1988 Spring seminar of the Arthur W. Page Society, New York.

5. *World Investment Report 1993*, published by United Nations Publications, and written and edited by the Division on Transnational Corporations and Investment of the United Nations Conference on Trade and Development.

6. Quote from an article by Secretary of Commerce Ronald H. Brown, in the *Viewpoints* section of *The New York Times,* Sunday, May 8, 1994.

7. Which countries in the developing world are attracting the most foreign direct investment? The volume of all such investment flows between 1981 and 1992 (the latest year for which there is comprehensive data) was $280,534 million.

Ten Largest Host Developing Countries for Foreign Direct Investment

INFLOWS

(1981–1992 in millions of dollars)

	Host	1981	1985	1988	1992	Total
1	China	1,659	1,875	11,156	33,768	
2	Singapore	1,600	1,047	3,655	5,635	33,012
3	Mexico	2,835	491	2,594	5,366	28,992
4	Malaysia	1,265	695	–*	4,469	18,794
5	Brazil	2,520	1,348	2,969	1,454	17,752
6	Hong Kong	1,088	–*	2,627	1,918	14,665
7	Argentina	837	919	1,147	4,179	12,199
8	Thailand		–*	1,105	2,116	10,205
9	Egypt	753	1,178	1,190	–*	7,755
10	Nigeria	546	478	–*	897	5,183

Source: Data from *World Investment Report 1994.* *- indicates data not available. Taiwan would rank 10, but the United Nations does not keep records on Taiwan.

8. See Peter Fuhrman and Michael Schuman's article on India entitled, "Now we are our own masters," in *Forbes,* May 23, 1994. Also note that Forbes reporter Andrew Tanzer has written frequently and expertly about the rapid growth of the private sector across Asia and the region's most prominent entrepreneurs. An extensive review of the Asian situation, as well as a broad insight into the rising tycoons of the Third World, can be found in *Forbes,* July 17, 1995.

9. Arthur Zeikel at a July 29, 1992 symposium, sponsored by *American Heritage, Forbes,* and Merrill Lynch, with extracts published in a special report section in *Forbes.*

Chapter Three

1. Dean L. Buntrock, at a July 29, 1992, symposium sponsored by *American Heritage, Forbes,* and Merrill Lynch, with extracts published in a special report section in *Forbes.*

2. *World Investment Report 1994,* published by United Nations Publications, and written and edited by the Division on Transnational Corporations and Investment of the United Nations Conference on Trade and Development.

3. The International Institute of Finance, Inc., which represents more than 185 of the world's largest private financial institutions, estimated in a public report on April 19, 1995, that total net capital flows to emerging economies reached $174.4 billion in 1974, with private finance accounting for almost 90% of the total and with official finance, mostly from such institutions as the International Monetary Fund and aid agencies.

4. Numerous investment banks and international organizations have produced estimates on global infrastructure outlays, with some of the best research having been done by the World Bank and published in various of its sectoral studies, as well as its annual *World Development Report,* published by Oxford University Press.

5. For an in-depth perspective on the global power situation see speeches by Anthony A. Churchill, former Director of Energy & Industry at the World Bank, notably: "Geopolitics of the Privatization of Power," at the Western Coal Transportation Association conference in Denver in September 1992; "Energy Demand and Supply in the Developing World, 1990-2020," at the World Bank Annual Conference on Development in 1993; and "Energy Financing: An Institutional Challenge," at the Pacific/Asia Energy Financing Forum in Hong Kong in November 1993.

6. George Hill, worldwide managing partner of Anderson Consulting's Utilities Industry Practice Writing Outlook, in Volume 4, 1994, the magazine of Anderson Consulting, & Co.

7. 1994 Annual Report of the International Finance Corporation (IFC), the private sector affiliate of the World Bank, Washington DC.

8. 1991 Annual Report of the International Finance Corporation (IFC), the private sector affiliate of the World Bank, Washington, DC.

9. See also *Forbes,* July 17, 1995, for articles on the world's richest people.

10. *McKinsey Quarterly* 1994, Number 1, published by the management consulting company, McKinsey & Co., headquartered in New York.

11. 1994, special sponsored section in *Institutional Investor* magazine, developed by the authorities and businesses in Hong Kong.

12. The concept of a multipolar world, as described in this book, originated in a speech by then World Bank President A.W. Clausen entitled, "Global Interdependence in the 1980s," presented to the Yomiuri International Economic Society, in Tokyo, January 13, 1982. One of the lead economists at the World Bank to develop this perspective on global economic development with A.W. Clausen was S.J. Burki, now the World Bank's Vice-President for Latin America and the Caribbean.

Chapter Four

1. See Bertrand Russell, *The History of Western Philosophy.*

2. Research in Gansu, China, was undertaken by author Frank Vogl in 1991.

3. Nicholas D. Kristoff, "The Rise of China," in *Foreign Affairs* magazine, November/December,1993, published by the Council on Foreign Relations, New York.

4. Meeting on May 26, 1983, at the Great Hall of the People, Beijing, with Deng Xiaoping and a World Bank delegation including, World Bank President A.W. Clausen, Vice-President Attila Karaosmanoglu, Economist for China Edward Lim, Division Chief for China Caio Koch-Weser, and then Director of Information & Public Affairs Frank Vogl.

5. *China:The Next Economic Superpower,* published by Weidenfeld & Nicholson, London (and published as *The Rise of China* by W.W. Norton & Company, New York), by William Overholt, Managing Director of Bankers Trust, Hong Kong.

6. *Chemical Week* magazine, New York, August 31/September 7, 1994.

7. Life expectancy at birth doubled from less than 35 years in the early 1950s to 70 years at present; crude death rates and infant mortality fell by more than 75%, and illiteracy declined from 80% of the adult population in the early 1950s to about 30% at present.

The dynamism of the big coastal Chinese cities gets much foreign attention, but it would be a mistake to overlook the fundamental changes taking place in rural China, with its population of nearly 900 million. Average incomes here more than doubled in the 1980s and may well double again this decade. Infant and child mortality has declined sharply. Universal education of five years was achieved, and legislation was approved to move toward nine years compulsory education for all. The gains in farm output seen in the 1980s were coupled with 22 percent annual growth in rural manufacturing and services. The decade saw a shift of more than 60 million farm laborers from the unproductive make-work environment that characterized China's agricultural sector prior to decollectivization to the dynamic rural non-farm sectors.

Investment averaged 31 percent of gross domestic product in the early 1980s and 38 percent since 1985. Industrialization increased the international competitiveness of China's exports, and merchandise exports grew from $18.3 billion in 1980 to $52 billion in 1990. The opening of China's economy to the international market is a reform that rivals the transformation in agriculture. In 1990, trade amounted to nearly 17.4 percent of GNP, compared to 4.5 percent in 1980.

Data here is drawn from materials provided to author Frank Vogl by government ministries in Beijing in 1992 and from the China Department of the World Bank.

8. Marvin Whaley, president of McDonald's China operations, in *Financial Times,* February, 1995.

Chapter Five

1. Much of the data used on individual country economic conditions is drawn from the "World Economic Indicators" section of the "World Development

Report 1994," compiled by the World Bank and published by Oxford University Press. Also see the Asian Development Bank's Asian Development Outlook 1995 and 1996, published by Oxford University Press, and the Annual Report 1994 of the Asian Development Bank.

2. See *The East Asian Miracle: Economic Growth and Public Policy*, A World Bank Policy Research Report, 1993, Oxford University Press.

3. James Sinclair spends several months in India each year and maintains a home near Bangalore. He has travelled extensively in India over the last dozen years. Frank Vogl visited numerous times while he was an official at the World Bank.

4. World Bank Vice President for South Asia, Joe Wood, noted at a business conference in Tokyo on May 9, 1995, that: "Within an overall population of 900 million, India's consumer market is large and growing. The middle class is approximately 150 million. These people own or rent their own homes, have bank and credit card accounts, travel, have their own means of transportation, and work in white collar, service-oriented jobs. Along with this educated, largely urban-based consumer class, which is expected to double in size over the next decade or so, there has been a gradual improvement in the standard of living among the 70 percent of Indians who live in rural areas . . . per capita income throughout India has been growing by two percent a year for the past 15 years. Based on the reforms, we are now forecasting an acceleration of the growth rate to 3.5 percent a year for the next 15 years."

5. In the same speech in Tokyo, the World Bank's Joe Wood also stressed that India, with its size and financial savings rate in excess of 13 percent of gross domestic product, "has a financial sector that is far more sophisticated than in other countries at comparable levels of per capita income. It has a well-developed legal system, an independent judiciary, and a free press. In the context of a reform scenario, the package that India offers is difficult to match

in other developing countries."

6. See "Making Haste in India," an article in *Infrastructure Finance* magazine by Eapen Thomas, February/March 1994. Since that article, the project has progressed, although some political difficulties remain that could cause some delays.

7. *The Economist,* "A Survey of Vietnam," July 8, 1995.

Chapter Six

1. Note, in particular, the 1994 and 1995 annual reports, before and after the Mexican crisis, published by the World Bank and the Inter-American Development Bank. While both were optimistic on Mexico and the region in 1994, both continued to highlight the scale of reforms seen in the region, the progress that has been made, and the very bright outlook after the Mexican crisis.

2. See *The Christian Science Monitor,* May 11, 1994.

3. See Howard W. French, "Out of South Africa, Progress," in *The New York Times,* July 6, 1995, which provided many examples of South African enterprises already making substantial direct investments throughout much of southern and eastern Africa, as well as in parts of western Africa. The prime investment sectors have so far been mining, tourism, and railways.

4. *Foreign Direct Investment in Africa,* published on July 4, 1995, by the United Nations. This is the first comprehensive analysis of flows of foreign direct investment to sub-Saharan Africa. It was undertaken by the Division on Transnational Corporations and Investment at the United Nations Conference on Trade and Development (UNCTAD).

Chapter Seven

1. Quotes from the *Financial Times,* July 4, 1995, on statements made by the EBRD president in Moscow on the previous day. Mr. de Larosière has been one of the outstanding and most astute figures in international public finance for a generation, having served as the most senior French Treasury official

for international economic policy for many years in the 1970s, as Managing Director of the International Monetary Fund for a decade, as Governor of the Banque de France and, since 1993, as President, European Bank for Reconstruction and Development

2. *OECD Economic Outlook 57,* June 1995, published by the Organization for Economic Cooperation and Development, Paris.

3. *China: The Next Economic Superpower,* published by Weidenfeld & Nicholson, London (and published as *The Rise of China* by W.W. Norton & Company, New York), by William Overholt, Managing Director of Bankers Trust, Hong Kong.

4. *Forbes,* August 1994, story on business conditions in Russia.

5. *OECD Economic Outlook 57.*

6. *OECD Economic Outlook 57.*

7. The IMF publishes an analysis of global economic prospects twice each year. Created in 1946, the IMF is the international organization most responsible for providing financial resources in emergency situations to countries with acute balance of payments problems. Located in Washington DC, the IMF, in its first 30 years, was mainly involved in managing the world's currency system and assisting the leading industrial countries. Since then, however, its main focus has been the emerging economies. For example, in early 1995 it mobilized $17.8 billion as part of an emergency rescue package for Mexico. The IMF borrows its resources from its member governments: Almost all nations are members, but the most powerful, led by the United States and Japan, have the greatest influence.

8. "The OECD Jobs Study," published in June 1994, by the Organization for Economic Cooperation and Development (member countries are Canada, the United States, Japan, Belgium, Denmark, France, Germany, Greece, Iceland, Italy, Luxembourg, Netherlands, Portugal, Spain, United Kingdom, Turkey, Austria, Finland, Iceland, Norway, Sweden, Switzerland, Australia, and New Zealand). OECD is a research organization for governments and a forum for leaders of member countries to review a full array of economic policies.

Chapter Eight

1. Yoichi Funabashi, Washington DC bureau chief of the Asahi Shimbun of Japan, writing on "The Asianization of Asia" in *Foreign Affairs,* November/December 1993, published by the Council on Foreign Relations, New York.

2. These leaders have stressed frequently, both in major public speeches and media interviews, that they are searching for policies that promote capitalism with a human face. Prior to coming to power, they held socialist convictions, although they rejected the Moscow version of socialism. They recognized, on assuming the leadership of their countries, that modernization would only be possible within an open, free enterprise environment. Their efforts have been directed at creating firm foundations for democracy and winning respect for policies that offer the prospect of thriving business development yielding resources that can sustain state managed social welfare programs.

3. The Bolivian capitalization was announced in 1994 and started to be implemented in the first half of 1995.

4. See the special section on social responsibility codes in the United Nations Conference on Trade and Development's *World Development Report 1994,* August 1994.

5. See the special section on social responsibility codes in the United Nations Conference on Trade and Development's *World Development Report 1994,* August 1994.

6. See the special section on social responsibility codes in the United Nations Conference on Trade and Development's *World Development Report 1994,* August 1994.

7. See *Journey* volume 7, number 2, September 1993. *Journey* is the magazine of the Coca-Cola Company.

8. See the special section on social responsibility codes in the United Nations Conference on Trade and Development's *World Development Report 1994,* August 1994.

Chapter Nine

1. Lord Young, in a BBC World Service interview in May 1994 in which the issue of the tax deductibility of bribes paid abroad by European multinational corporations was one of the themes.
2. The EBRD, based in London and owned by the governments of Europe, Canada, Japan, and the United States, exists to further economic development, especially private sector development, in the former communist Warsaw Pact countries of Eastern and Central Europe. Its *Annual Economic Report,* published in September 1993, devoted considerable space to reporting on progress in privatization in the region and stressed the major corrosive impact of corruption.
3. George Moody-Stewart, booklet on "Grand Corruption," published by Transparency International, Berlin, Germany. Peter Eigen, a German national, worked for the World Bank for 25 years before taking early retirement in 1992 to devote his full energies to establishing and leading TI. Author Frank Vogl, who worked with Eigen in the 1980s at the World Bank, is one of two vice-chairmen of TI, with the other vice-chairman being Kamal Hosain, former foreign minister and justice minister of Bangladesh.
5. Michael Hershman, one of the founders of Transparency International and a member of its Board of Directors, described the changing attitudes of official authorities towards money laundering at the TI launch conference in Berlin in May 1993

Chapter Ten

1. See the March 1994 article by economists Vivek B. Arora and Tamim A. Bayoumi in *Finance & Development,* the quarterly journal of the International Monetary Fund and the World Bank, available free from these Washington DC-based institutions.
2. United Nations Development Program's "Human Development Report 1994," published by Oxford University Press provides a broad overview of trends

in military spending in the Third World.
3. See *The Brookings Review,* Spring 1994.
4. See "A Conversation with Lee Kuan Yew," by Fareed Zakaria, in *Foreign Affairs* magazine, March/April 1994, published by the Council on Foreign Relations.
5. The annual *Human Resources Report* of the United Nations Development Program, the *State of the World's Children Report* by UNICEF, and the reports on *Social Indicators* and *World Economic Indicators* by the World Bank are among numerous regular studies that provide detailed information on the countries that have secured meaningful social and economic progress and those that have yet to move ahead. These reports show, for example, the scale of social progress in even in some of the poorest countries on earth:

- Life expectancy has increased from 53 years to 62 years since 1970;
- Infant mortality has decreased from 110 per 1,000 births in 1970 to 73 per 1,000;
- Income: gross national product per capita advanced from $190 in 1975 to $390;
- Access to safe water over the last 20 years has more than doubled to almost 70 percent;
- Primary school enrollment in the last 20 years had increased by 36 percent;
- Globally, immunization against measles, one of the main childhood killers, has risen from around 50 percent in 1985 to more than 70 percent.

Chapter Eleven

1. George Grune in the 1989 commencement address at the Roy E. Crummer Graduate School of Business in Florida.
2. See "SPIN DRY Asia is the last phase in Whirlpool's global wash cycle," by Gregory E. David, *Forbes,* October 26, 1993.
3. *World Investment Report 1994.*
4. Interesting aspects of the marketing impact of the joint Sandoz-Gerber are described in "Sandoz opens world for Gerber," in *Advertising Age,* May 30, 1994.

5. See survey results and articles by Peter Martin and Paul Taylor, in the *Financial Times,* June 27, 1994.

Chapter Twelve

1. AT&T's increasing focus on global opportunities is noted in its 1993 and 1994 annual reports.
2. See "Gold Rush—Job of Wiring China Sets Off Wild Scramble By the Telecom Giants," by John J. Keller and Marcus W. Brauchli in the *Wall Street Journal,* April 5, 1994.
3. Presentation by David Frost, entitled, "International Privatizations, Business Development, and Investment Opportunities," at a July 15, 1993, AT&T symposium called: Global Telecommunications: A Strategic Advantage.
4. 1994 Annual Report of the International Finance Corporation, the private sector affiliate of the World Bank, Washington DC, which was created in 1956 and has become a leading source of private finance for joint ventures in developing countries.

Chapter Thirteen

1. "U.S. Manufacturers in the Global Marketplace—A Research Report," by The Conference Board, Report Number 1058-94-RR.
2. "U.S. Manufacturers in the Global Marketplace—A Research Report," by The Conference Board, Report Number 1058-94-RR.
3. *Capability and character in global finance,* published as a brochure by J.P. Morgan, New York, 1993.
4. See "Behind VW's stunning U.S. decline," by Raymond Serafin, *Advertising Age,* September 13, 1993.

Chapter Fourteen

1. Some of the information in this section is based on the firsthand experience of Frank Vogl, who was hired by Michael Nelson in 1967 in London as a trainee reporter in the Reuters economic news services.

2. See the 1993 and 1994 annual reports of WPP Group plc.
3. Interview published in an article entitled, "Coat of Many Colors: Benetton Weaves Diversity Into a Global Marketing Phenomenon," in *Outlook* 1994, the magazine of Andersen Consulting.

Chapter Fifteen

1. See "Toys 'R' Us: Can Foreign Sales Restore the Lazarus Luster?" in *Barron's,* September 27, 1993.
2. See "Globalization Holds the Key," a full-page advertisement by Hitachi, in the *Financial Times,* September 17, 1993.
3. See "Global Perspective Provides Competitive Edge," a full-page advertisement by Toshiba, in the *Financial Times,* June 27, 1994.
4. The *Financial Times,* June 27, 1994, full page advertisement by Toshiba under the heading of "Global Perspective Provides Competitive Edge."
5. The *Financial Times.....*

Chapter Sixteen

1. See American Express Annual Report 1994, and "Reshaping the Organization-The American Express Experience," remarks by Harvey Golub, chairman and CEO of the American Express Company, New York University Stern School of Business, March 7, 1995.
2. See "Meeting the challenge of the future: A new look at the Japanese trading company," by Minoru Makihara, president and CEO of Mitsubishi Corporation, in *Andersen Consulting's Outlook* magazine, Spring 1994.
3. See "A Global Citizen For A Global McKinsey," *Business Week,* April 11, 1994.
4. See Coca-Cola's 1993 Annual Report.
5. A fascinating introduction to some hands-on international public relations work is provided by Carole M. Howard at a Conference Board meeting in January 1992. Howard's address was entitled, "Perestroika from Pleasantville : Lessons Learned Launching Reader's Digest In The Soviet Union and Hungary."

Chapter Seventeen

1. Rupert Murdoch in an interview with *Advertising Age* magazine in June 1994.
2. Murdoch paid $ 1.6 billion to get the rights for Fox to broadcast the U.S. National Football League and then dramatically struck at CBS by paying $ 500 million to acquire 12 of its affiliated stations—actions that typified his aggressive approach.
3. Survey in October 1992 by Deloitte Touche Tohmatsu International, entitled, "Why Companies Go International-International Strategy of Middle Market Companies."
4. John Wybrew, Planning and Public Affairs Director, Shell U.K. Limited, in an occasional Paper on "Global forces for change—the challenge to U.K. business and society," from Business in The Community's Work in Society seminars 1993-94 and a seminar for the Corporate Responsibility Group, entitled, "Educating for What?"
5. See "Facilitating Foreign Investment," by Louis T. Wells, Jr. and Alvin G. Wint, Occasional Paper 2, 1991, published by the Foreign Investment Advisory Service, a division jointly sponsored by two World Bank affiliates—the International Finance Corporation and the Multilateral Investment Guarantee Agency.
6. The European Union, formerly named the European Community, founded in 1957 from the base of the European Coal and Steel Community and expanded over time to now embrace 15 countries, is the largest trading bloc in the world. It will expand as more East European countries join, and it will strengthen, over time, as efforts to unify the European currencies and establish a common economic policy increase.

   ASEAN, the Association of South-East Asian Countries, founded in 1967, is of growing importance and may well, in time, evolve into a close collaboration with other Asia countries and with the United States.

   NAFTA, the North American Freed Trade Agreement, came into effect in 1994 between Canada, the U.S., and Mexico as an expansion from the Canadian-U.S. free trade agreement of 1989.

   The **Andean Pact**, (founded 1969), the Central American Common Market (founded 1961) and the Latin American Free Trade Area (founded in 1960), are some of the Latin American arrangements that have had differing degrees of success. Linkages with NAFTA over time may strengthen each of them significantly.

   The **Economic Community of West African States** (founded in 1975) and the Preferential Trade Area for Eastern and Southern Africa (founded in 1987) are two of an array of African trade arrangements that have had differing degrees of success.

Chapter Eighteen

1. The major think tanks have all developed strengths in the international economic domain. Some, like the Brookings Institution in Washington D.C. and the London Business School, are homes for some of the world's leading economists and experts on foreign countries. These experts are often available for consultation and, in effect, for the verification of knowledge secured through other sources. Some of the think tanks have developed excellent lists of contacts that can be of value to the corporation going global. For example, John Yochelson, a senior executive at the Center for Strategic and International Studies in Washington D.C., has, over the last 15 years, developed an impressive number of specialist conferences on a broad array of international business topics. Yochelson has, in the process, built an enviable list of contacts in many areas, and he and his CSIS colleagues today represent a significant source of information on current international business developments.

Chapter Twenty

1. Study by the UNCTAD Division on Transnational Corporations, September 1993, entitled "Small and Medium-Sized

Transnational Corporations: Role, Impact, and Policy Implications." The study, based largely on a survey of hundreds of SMEs in manufacturing and services sectors in 18 industrial countries, showed that approximately two-thirds of all foreign direct investments by SMEs have taken place in the last dozen years. SMEs, defined as companies with less than 500 employees in their home countries, account for more than one-half of the total share of employment, sales, and value added in most countries. The report stated that SMEs are a major driving force of national economies. The study highlighted the importance of SMEs, the trends in their international investment patterns, the changing attitudes among managers of SMEs towards international investment, and factors that enable SMEs to compete effectively in foreign markets with large transnational corporations.

2. Sutton Resources Ltd. is a minerals exploration company based in Richmond, British Columbia. James Sinclair is Chairman and Frank Vogl is a member of the Board of Directors of this company, which is quickly amassing substantial nickel, cobalt, copper, and gold assets. It aims to become a significant international minerals production company.

3. See the coverage in Chapter 19 on approaches to negotiation by Roman Shklanka.

4. The actions undertaken by Sutton coincided with philanthropic work by James Sinclair and his family in Tanzania in the areas of healthcare, the environment, and village economic development. A foundation was established, directed by James and Barbara Sinclair's eldest daughter, Marlene Sinclair, who became a resident of Tanzania and whose prime project was the establishment of an orphanage and hospice center for AIDS victims.

Index